Forgotten Tales
of Carson Valley
and Nearby Settlements

Karen Dustman

Warm thanks to the Douglas County Historical Society & Museum and Dangberg Home Ranch Historic Park for permission to reprint the special photographs included in this volume. These historic photos really bring the stories to life. Thank you so much for allowing us to share them!

Grateful thanks are also due to Wally Adams, Gail Allen, Teri Balfour, Dale Bohlman, Bob Ellison, Michael Fischer, Krista Jenkins and the Thran/Cordes families, Mark Jensen, Debbe Nye, Billie Rightmire, Marge Shively, Sue Silver, Marilyn Summers, and Judy Wickwire for photos, information, and help with these stories.

And a very special thanks to Judy Conrad, whose enthusiasm was the spark that lit the fire under this book!

First Edition

Copyright 2019 - Karen Dustman
All Rights Reserved

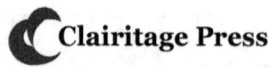
Clairitage Press

Printed in the United States

Table of Contents

Chapter 1: Landmarks & Places 5

Chapter 2: Ranchers & Local Folk 63

Chapter 3: Wild Men & Wild Times 96

Chapter 4: Buried Treasure & A Bit of Romance ... 121

Index 152

Introduction

These stories grew from our rambles through Carson Valley and its surrounding area. Every outing produced so many questions! What was that fascinating old building all about? Who used to live over there? One by one, we dug out the stories and shared what we'd found in our local history newsletter and blog.

Almost before we knew it, these history stories had morphed into a book. *This* book, to be precise. Because people kept telling us how much they loved reading them. And because all good stories need a place to be saved and cherished, so they can easily be found and read again.

We hope you enjoy these tales of days gone by. Even more, we hope they help you discover the traces of those early pioneers and "early days" that still remain here in beautiful Carson Valley.

Chapter 1

LANDMARKS & PLACES

THE OLD CARSON VALLEY CREAMERY

This mysterious building on Waterloo Lane used to be something. Carson Valley folks have probably driven by it dozens of times, wondering: what's its story?

Back in the day — 1891, to be precise — this used to be the Carson Valley Creamery. And not just *any* creamery, mind you; this was a gold-medal-winning local creamery!

What got the whole creamery notion rolling was a series of letters to Carson Valley's E. Cohn from a man in L.A. The writer just happened to run a creamery in Los Angeles for Lucky Baldwin. (Don't know who Lucky Baldwin was? I didn't either. His real name was Elias Jackson Baldwin (born 1828); the "lucky" moniker came from his extraordinarily good luck at wheeling and dealing. *Wikipedia* calls Baldwin "one of the greatest pioneers" in California business; he built San Francisco's posh Baldwin Hotel & Theatre, and bought up so much Southern California land that his name still lives on there. Check out the *Wikipedia* article on Baldwin; well worth a glance!)

Chapter 1 - Landmarks/Places

As for those letters – well, it was something like receiving a missive from Bill Gates. When Bill Gates tells you creameries are a grand business, you have to at least consider it!

A meeting of local farmers was speedily convened at Valhalla Hall in March, 1891, to discuss the idea. C.C. Henningsen explained the relatively simple concept to the group: each dairy farmer would put his own marked milk cans out by the road; a creamery wagon would pick them up and haul them to the creamery; skim milk could be returned to the farmers in their own cans for a small price. By selling and shipping their butter and cheese collectively, it was hoped the farmers could reach larger markets and get a better price. H. Springmeyer immediately came out as an advocate for the plan.

The newspaper was jammed with "Creamery Talk" that whole spring and summer. Before long, a two story, 36 x 86-foot building was being erected on a ten-acre parcel at the southeast corner of William Dangberg's ranch. Plans for the new building called for a cold storage area, a butter room, and a separator room on the ground floor; plus an "ice room" that spanned both floors. Upstairs would be the cheese room, kitchen, dining room and three "chambers."

The old Creamery, nestled in the trees - a quintessential Carson Valley scene.

In July, 1891, the creamery group signed a five-year contract with Julius Kaupisch and his brother, both trained at a dairy school in Saxony, Germany. One Kaupisch brother promptly set off for Chicago to procure machinery. A steam engine was purchased and hauled in from a former steam laundry in Carson City, and a 90-foot well was drilled by George Hawkins to supply the new creamery with fresh water.

Corporate officers for the new enterprise included John Frantzen as president and C.M. Henningsen as Secretary. Banker and man-of-many-talents Fritz Heise not only served as the company's treasurer but also helpfully hauled rock for the new creamery's foundation. C.E. Merrick hired on as the manager.

"The farmers are enthusiastic over the subject and are preparing to milk as many cows as possible," the newspaper boasted, adding that local dairymen were scouting for good stock to add to their herds. "In a few years this Valley will be stocked with the finest lot of milk cows to be found anywhere."

To expand local herds supplying the creamery, the Kaupisch brothers brokered the purchase of another 360 cows from dairies near the California coast that were shutting down — a whole trainload. In the process, though, the Kaupisch pair managed to royally trample on a few local feelings; the new cows were mostly Jerseys, Durhams, and Short Horns, because (the Kaupisch brothers claimed) Holsteins "do not prove to be good milkers."

This last comment received an agitated response in the local *Appeal* newspaper: "The Kaupisch Brothers, if they made such a statement, evidently know little about milch cows," the writer sniffed. "Let the proprietors of the Carson Valley Creamery investigate the records of thoroughbreds and not take the products of halfbreeds as a standard."

The ramp where milk cans were delivered. (Courtesy of Douglas County Historical Society & Museum).

The new creamery was touted as a win-win-win for local farmers: "Instead of hunting a market for their butter, they can remain at home and give their full attention to the farm and dairy work," the local newspaper cheered. "There is no longer need for importing cheese from other States, for a choice article in this line will be manufactured" right there at the new creamery. And the more Carson Valley hay that local dairymen purchased to feed their growing herds, "the more you are patronizing home industry and assisting in making your own community self-supporting." It was downright patriotic to patronize the creamery!

Chapter 1 - Landmarks/Places

When the new creamery building was up and running in the fall of 1891, it had machinery able to handle milk from up to 3,000 cows, and promised production of up to 1.5 tons of butter and 3 tons of cheese each and every day. Milk was to be delivered to the creamery twice a day in summer, and once a day in winter months, and farmers were promised $1 per hundred pounds of milk to start (provided that it tested at four pounds of butter to the hundred-weight).

Mural inside Katie's Restaurant at Carson Valley Inn shows rancher Herman Scheele, on his way from Fredericksburg to the Creamery with more than 30 cans of milk.

A visiting reporter from the *Genoa Weekly Courier* gave a fascinating overview of the operation in July, 1891. Farmers would deliver ten-gallon cans of milk, each weighing roughly 80 pounds. Cream content was tested once a month for each farm, and every batch of incoming milk was tested, too, to be sure it hadn't been watered or skimmed.

The incoming milk was dumped into an immense bucket for weighing; then the bucket was hoisted to the upper story and drained into a large vat, where pipes took the milk to a centrifugal separator. And not just any separator, mind you; this separator was a special gem, imported from Germany and known as the "Alexandra."

Once the Alexandra had done its work, the skimmed milk was returned to cans for farmers wishing to buy it (at ten cents per hundred pounds), or drained into the cheese tank for reuse. Watching one such operation, the newspaper reported that farmers "had the skimmed milk in the cans

A milk delivery. (Courtesy Douglas County Historical Society & Museum).

and were ready to return home" just twenty minutes after the milk had been delivered.

The butter and cheese operations were additional marvels. Cream was conveyed from the giant Alexandra separator to a cream vat for cooling, where it was allowed to rest or "ripen" for 24 hours before being sent off one of two steam-driven churns, holding 400 gallons each. A six-foot circular "butter worker" table came next, where salt was added and the butter got worked over by rollers. Off to the cold storage room it went, where it was molded into two-pound square blocks and then packed into cases of 120 pounds apiece. Shipments of butter went to Carson three times a week.

A separate cheese-making operation produced small and large rings of cheese, weighing 9 and 28 pounds respectively; as many as 200 of these were turned out a day. (The secret to turning skimmed milk into fatty cheese, shared later by a worker: the addition of just the right proportion of lard!) From the curing room, cheese wheels would slide down a convenient chute into a waiting wagon and were whisked off to market. As for the butter, that was packed into wooden crates, shipped by wagon to Carson City, then loaded onto trains for Virginia City and San Francisco.

And a lucky thing all that hauling that proved to be for teamster Fritz Dangberg. Dangberg arrived from Germany in 1895, and quickly got hired on by the Creamery to drive teams to Carson City. While in Carson, Dangberg used to stable his horses with Zirn Andersen, at Andersen's Hay Yard. And there, as luck would have it, Dangberg got to know Zirn's sister-in-law, Metta Winkelman, who was staying with the Andersens. One thing led to another, and Fritz and Metta were married in 1897.

Chapter 1 - Landmarks/Places

Judy Wickwire photo

THE DAKE HOUSE

This beautiful old home on the south end of Genoa just screams Victorian, doesn't it?

This is the Dake House, and it's now listed on the National Register of Historic Places. It is also said to be one of the "most-haunted" sites in Nevada! And there's a really good reason why a few ghosts might be hanging around....

Charles W. Dake was the local undertaker in Genoa for many years (although he formally listed his occupation as "carpenter" in the 1880 census). He not only built coffins but other things as well – including this house.

Dake's advertisement as undertaker, Genoa Weekly Courier, *June 5, 1885.*

Born in Canada, Dake initially settled in Alpine County, California when he came to the west coast in the 1860s. In 1866 he was living in the silver mining boomtown of Silver Mountain City. He became a supervisor and served as Chairman of the Board in 1868-69. One son,

Charles, was born in 1869 while he and his wife lived in Silver Mountain. By the time of the 1870 census Dake had moved his family to Monitor, where he found a job as superintendent for the mill at the Globe Mine. Of his five offspring, the four younger children were all listed on the census as having been born in California – likely Alpine County.

Dake (like everyone else in the vicinity at the time) invested in the local mines and (like far too many) got cross-wise with mine promoter Lewis Chalmers. Chalmers tried to buy Dake's interest in the Extenuate Mine in the 1870s, but Dake refused to sell unless he first saw cash in hand. (Smart man!) In one particularly funny letter to his associates in London, Chalmers complained that another local miner had cautioned Dake to "sign nothing with us . . . [he said] we are bilks, and so forth." And, well, if the shoe fits. . . .

Chalmers did eventually manage to buy Dake's shares. But he only accomplished that feat by using a straw man (someone Dake trusted) to make the purchase.

Dake departed from Monitor about 1872, after the Globe Mine was shut down "temporarily." Like so many eager miners, he probably realized the mine would never be profitable and moved on, seeking greener pastures.

Dake purchased his property here in Genoa about 1872. And, being a carpenter, Dake is said to have built the house himself! But he wasn't the first person to live at this site.

This structure is believed to have replaced an earlier log cabin. Harry Hawkins notes in his oral history that an old African-American man was said to have lived here originally. When the man died, he was buried just to the north and a rock fence was built later, right over his grave. So that might explain why at least *one* irritable ghost would still occupy this property.

Charles Dake kept his undertaking parlor (now gone) in a separate building, located on the north side of this house. Over the years Dake's Victorian home served as a post office and as his office as Justice of the Peace. An old barn and carriage house also still stand on the property.

Chapter 1 - Landmarks/Places

As we've mentioned, among the many hats he wore, Dake served as Justice of the Peace in the 1890s. One of the more interesting court cases he handled was the trial of a man named L.T. Franklin, in the spring of 1898. Franklin had been charged with practicing "medicine and surgery" without benefit of a medical diploma.

A trial was set and a full jury assembled. The witnesses and attorneys were all there, ready for the trial. But Judge Dake entered his courtroom that morning and summarily dismissed the case. According to the local paper, "the Justice was not at all certain that a jury could be obtained in this township that would convict the defendant." Dr. Franklin was evidently doing such a good job practicing medicine, none of the locals were willing to stop him, diploma or not!

A second court case involving Dake just goes to show that opioid problems aren't exactly a new thing; they had them, even back in 1898. In this instance, the Genoa town constable had caught someone dead to rights in the act of smoking an opium pipe at the very time

> ·Constable Gray arrested an Indian Wednesday night for smoking opium. The Indian had his trial yesterday in Justice Dake's court and was sentenced to ten days in jail. The Indian was smoking at the time of his arrest and the Constable captured his pipe, which was afterwards destroyed as the law requires.

Dake's verdict was reported in the Genoa Weekly Courier, *April 22, 1898.*

of his arrest. It was pretty hard to argue with those facts. The defendant was arrested and hauled before Justice Dake, who sentenced him to serve ten days in jail. And the man lost his opium pipe into the bargain, too. So that gives you an idea of the kinds of cases that Dake, as Justice of the Peace, was called upon to hear.

The Dake home was eventually sold in 1909 to Theodore and Clara Hawkins. Clara reportedly planted the lilac bushes, snowball bushes, and fruit trees you can still see around the property today.

Dake's undertaking parlor has now disappeared. But it once had an exciting journey. In July, 1891, a heavy cloudburst washed the entire building down the hill and into the fields below owned by the Frey family, and there are tales about coffins coming down into the field along with it. Those sturdy, no-nonsense old-timers simply dragged the wooden building back up to its earlier spot, and put it up on a replacement foundation. When the building was finally demolished for good in 1958, it's said they found dried mud still packed between the floor joists.

And what kinds of ghostly encounters have been reported at the Dake House? Well, *lots* of them!

Staff members working at the antique store have reported "phantom shadows." (Doesn't that kinda give you goosebumps?) The ghostly figure of an older woman has been spotted lurking around the first floor, and some visitors claim to have detected the odor of sweet perfume in the parlor.

People downstairs have heard footsteps tromping around over their heads, even when nobody was upstairs. One visitor to the master bedroom on the second floor claims he felt a distinct slap as if someone had hit him on the face – although no one else was there in the room at the time.

Perhaps the most often-told ghost story of all at the Dake House involves a painting. It looks like an ordinary enough oil painting: a vase with a bunch of roses in it. But the painting has an interesting history. It is said to be an original or copy of a "spirit painting" done by a medium during a seance over in San Francisco.

According to local lore, the owner of the antique store tried to sell the mysterious painting three separate times. Each time, the painting would "violently plunge off the wall." One time it hit an electrical plug on its way down, sending up a cascade of sparks.

The "Spirit Painting" would plunge off the wall. (Illustration by Karen Dustman).

Chapter 1 - Landmarks/Places

Interestingly enough, each time it fell, no damage was caused to the painting or its mounting. But three times of having it crash to the ground was enough to get the message across; the owner hasn't tried to sell the painting since.

Given that a former undertaking parlor once sat nearby, you can kinda understand why a few ghosts might be hanging around, right? And there are other explanations for possible ghosts in the home, as well.

As we've said, there was that African American man who once lived here and is buried on the north side of the house, with a rock wall sitting over his grave. That could make anyone just a little irritable, right?

THE SPIRIT

The current owner's mother also lived in the home for a time before she died. So that's could help explain the reported female spirit.

The spirit painting could have come from San Francisco with its own unsettled spirit attached. And of course there were all those bodies that passed through Dake's undertaking parlor over the years, and all the grieving friends and spouses who probably came to his home.

But that's not all. Dake's wife, Harriet, passed away in Genoa (possibly even here in this house) in September, 1878. The precise day she died? You guessed it: Friday the 13th.

As for C.W. Dake himself, he passed away at the age of 79 in November, 1908. Records show he is buried in a plot near the top of Genoa Cemetery, along with wife Harriet, son Bert, and five other Dakes.

Sadly, these family graves are currently unmarked. Like so many early ones, their headstones may once have been made of wood. There's even a local rumor that C.W. Dake's headstone might have been stolen, long ago. Or perhaps you might say it was — spirited away!

The Dake/Simonis plot at Genoa Cemetery (Judy Wickwire photo).

Chapter 1 - Landmarks/Places

Kingsbury Grade, circa 1895 - 1905.
(Photo courtesy of Douglas County Historical Society)

THE STORY OF
KINGSBURY GRADE (PART 1)

Few people ever stop to read the historic marker for Kingsbury Grade. Perhaps that's because the marker isn't actually on today's Kingsbury road at all but rather on Foothill, tucked between Mottsville and Muller Lanes. But this small sign marks a fascinating and important early site: the original jumping-off spot for emigrants bent on taking the Daggett Pass route to the goldfields of California.

It wasn't everyone's first choice as a route, though.

Long before white men arrived, this trail began as a simple Washoe footpath up to the lake. At the height of the Gold Rush, Georgetown (Calif.) boosters began working to press the track into service to draw emigrants to their community. These enterprising townsfolk sent "salesmen" over to the Eastern slope to divert would-be miners to Georgetown, instead of taking the usual Placerville route. These hired hawkers vigorously promoted what soon became known as the "Georgetown Cutoff," assuring emigrants (falsely) that it would slash their remaining trek to the goldfields by 50 miles or more.

But the Georgetown Trail or Cut-off (as it then was known) remained a barely-improved footpath. In July, 1850, emigrant Edmund Hinde took one look at the steep, rough climb and decided to stick with his original plan to follow the more-established Carson Canyon route. "On looking at the [Georgetown] road, we concluded to keep to the old one," he sighed.

The flat at the base of the trail did make a fine place for a party, however. Many eager gold-seekers who opted to take the difficult Georgetown route had simply abandoned their wagons, guns,

Today's Nevada historical marker at the foot of the original Kingsbury Grade.

and other personal possessions at the foot of the trail and forged ahead as "packers." Those piles of discarded belongings became a temptation to mischief. In his 1850 diary, Abner Blackburn recounts how the boys of Mormon Station would go on a "spree," setting fire to piles of abandoned wagons, cutting up discarded harnesses, bending guns around trees, and "run[ning] amuck generally."

In 1852, J.H. Scott and his brothers had settled at the foot of the trail, building a small log cabin there. The location was a good one:

Chapter 1 - Landmarks/Places

it had a spring, and was only a few miles south of Mormon Station. The following year, the Scotts sold out to Dr. Charles Daggett. Born in Vermont in 1806, Dr. Charles Daggett had come west in 1851. According to local lore, Daggett brought two African-American slaves with him to Carson Valley, a woman and her little boy, thus becoming one of the very few early slave-holders in the valley.

Daggett and his companions settled into the log cabin at the base of the mountain. His land claim, filed May 12, 1853 for 640 acres, was among the earliest in the "First Records." In 1854, Daggett solidified his claim by having a survey made of his property. A graduate of Berkshire Medical College in Massachusetts, Daggett was the first doctor in the region and, by some accounts, the first in all of future Nevada. He also held public posts in 1855 as Carson County Assessor/Tax Collector as well as its prosecuting attorney. Not surprisingly, the trail up the mountain near his home, the creek that flowed down the mountain, and the pass above all soon took his name.

And a lucky thing Dr. Daggett's presence was for Judge Orson Hyde, who arrived at Daggett's cabin with frostbitten feet and legs in December, 1855, after crossing the mountains in the snow. Aware of the potential tissue damage with rapid-thawing, Daggett chopped a hole in the ice on a nearby stream and told Hyde to soak his legs. He then rubbed Hyde's frozen legs with turpentine and bandaged them in soft cotton.

The very fortunate traveler, Orson Hyde.

For several more years, Daggett Trail remained practical only for travelers on foot or with pack-horses or mules. Surveyor George Goddard, visiting in 1855, noted that although the trail from top to bottom was just under four miles, the drop-off was steep and "a false step would precipitate one into the rocky canyon 500 feet below."

Then about 1856, a Genoa merchant named William Nixon took an interest in improving the Daggett route. A Mormon from St. Louis, Nixon had arrived in Genoa that year from Salt Lake with a load of goods with which he opened a store at Mormon Station. Before returning to Salt Lake in '57, Nixon had the trail over Daggett Pass improved so that wagons carrying goods had an easier time of it.

But "easier" was a relative term. In 1859, Capt. J.H. Simpson offered his own skeptical opinion that a great deal of work would be necessary to make the route truly passable by wagons.

The town of Genoa, as it appeared to Capt. J.H. Simpson and the U.S. Army Corps of Engineers in 1859. (National Archives).

For the most part, the Daggett route remained essentially a pack-mule or horse trail through most of the '50s. But the Comstock Lode would soon change all that.

Two ambitious businessmen (D.D. Kingsbury and John M. McDonald) saw huge profit potential in improving the road (and, of course, charging a hefty toll) to serve wagons laden with goods for the mines of Virginia City. They constructed the "Kingsbury & McDonald Toll Road" over Daggett Pass, beginning in the winter of 1859 and finishing in August, 1860.

It was an important step not only for Kingsbury and McDonald, but for Carson Valley itself. Writing in November, 1859, Richard Allen predicted the road project would "facilitate communication, reduce freight, and add materially to the advancement of Carson Valley." And right he was.

And there's more – keep reading for Part 2 of the Kingsbury Grade story!

Chapter 1 - Landmarks/Places

Kingsbury Grade, circa 1895 - 1905, with what might be a flume at center-right.
(Photo courtesy of Douglas County Historical Society)

THE STORY OF
KINGSBURY GRADE (PART 2)

Even before the Kingsbury & McDonald toll road was completed, the quasi-passable track began to attract attention. A telegraph line for the Humboldt & Salt Lake Telegraph Co. was strung along this route in late 1858, connecting Genoa with Placerville. And beginning in April or May, 1860, Pony Express riders began following the Kingsbury Grade trail, before completion of the telegraph lines a few months later made their work obsolete.

When Kingsbury & McDonald's new wagon road was officially finished in August, 1860, it was seven miles long but reportedly chopped the distance from Genoa to Placerville by some 15 miles, saving travelers a precious day's travel.

Writer Richard Allen marveled at the workmanship on the new road, describing it as a "most excellent road" winding over "seemingly impassable heights." A reporter for the *Sacramento Daily Union* similarly effused in June, 1860: "The road-building by McDonald & Kingsbury through Daggett's Pass is pronounced by those we have seen who have passed over it, the best on the Pacific coast."

The roadway of the new Kingsbury route averaged a luxurious sixteen feet in width — a vast improvement over portions of the Placerville road in El Dorado County, where sharp turns planked to a width of just eight feet made it difficult for six-mule teams to "keep the wheels on the timber."

A freight wagon.

Kingsbury and McDonald received a Territorial franchise for their toll road in 1861. The initial toll for a wagon drawn by four horses making a round-trip from Shingle Springs to Van Sickle's Station at the foot of old Kingsbury was $17.50. That hefty sum represented more than four days' wages for a humble miner. Even so, writer Richard Allen dubbed the new toll rate "reasonable."

The Kingsbury route soon drew away many of the westward-bound travelers who had previously crossed through Hope Valley and over Luther Pass. In addition, with Virginia City at its height, pack train operators bringing supplies eastward for the Comstock mines found the route profitable in the early 1860s. Some of those early packers settled in and became Nevada notables. Bob Fulstone, for example, a well-known dairy rancher near Carson City, recalled "packing mules" over Daggett Pass as a teenager. A. Schwarz, cheerful proprietor of the popular Genoa Brewery, also ran a pack train

Chapter 1 - Landmarks/Places

from Sacramento to Virginia City in his younger days, also probably following the Kingsbury route over Daggett Pass.

At the very foot of the new Kingsbury trail, Henry Van Sickle already had an existing station that he'd erected in 1857. This offered several amenities for emigrants and teamsters: a bar, a hotel, a blacksmith/wheelwright shop, and a store. Van Sickle quickly embraced the new Kingsbury route as good for business. He not only helped finance the new road but also served as its first toll-master. Although we don't know much about the original toll house, we do know it had a brick chimney, as that fell down during an earthquake in June, 1887.

Henry Van Sickle.

About halfway up the grade, travelers could also find another way-station, called "Peters Station." Here Richard Peters and his wife, Elizabeth, kept a three-story hotel where teamsters could enjoy a good, hot dinner and get a restful night's sleep for themselves and their horses before attempting the rest of the climb.

The new Kingsbury toll road didn't keep its competitive advantage for long, however. In November, 1863, the Lake Bigler Road was completed and began siphoning off traffic. This new road ran from Friday's Station (then "Small & Burke's") on the south shore of the lake through Spooner's Station and down Kings Canyon to Carson City. It not only crossed the Sierra some 200 feet lower than the Kingsbury-McDonald route but, more importantly, reportedly offered a slightly shorter trek to the Placerville road.

Some adventurous souls tried riding the flume down the canyon.

That didn't mean that all travelers abandoned the new Kingsbury route, of course. And in 1866, J.W. Haines found yet another helpful use for it, building a mile-long box flume to channel water down Kingsbury Canyon, later upgrading its original overlapping joints to an "abutting joint" model in 1868.

All told, the new Kingsbury & McDonald toll road cost its founders an astonishing $585,000 to build. And in 1863, after the Kings Canyon route opened as competition, Kingsbury generated only $190,000 in tolls. Even so, the new Kingsbury toll road continued to operate. By 1881, the <u>History of Nevada</u> would grandly claim that the Kingsbury toll road had "annually returned double its cost."

Perhaps this was pure puffery. Financial woes eventually forced Van Sickle, who had helped to finance the road, to foreclose on his mortgage and he wound up becoming its owner. For a time, it continued to operate as the Van Sickle Toll Road. But in 1889, Van Sickle sold the roadway to Douglas County for just $1,000. It now became a free road; the local newspaper happily advised readers that "no toll will be collected in the future."

> The county having purchased the Kingsbury grade, the same is now a public road, and no toll will be collected in future.

Notice of discontinuing tolls on Kingsbury grade, from Genoa Weekly Courier, *October 11, 1889.*

The lack of tolls made a big difference for commerce over the Grade. In February, 1890, for example, ranchers in Carson Valley were able to supply Folsom's logging camp at Lake Tahoe with beef, which they "hauled over the Kingsbury grade on hand-sleds." And in 1894, a Sacramento hauler estimated the cost of delivery at a mere one cent per pound, compared with the previous $1.25 per pound when the toll over Kingsbury was $22.

Given the road's unpaved surface, maintenance needs were constant. In summer, horsedrawn carts would sprinkle water along the roadway to settle the dust. In winter, sleds were used to pack the snow down into a roadway.

Horrific accidents on the steep grade were also common. In June, 1890, a man named Green lost his brake while descending Kings-

Chapter 1 - Landmarks/Places

bury grade with a six-horse team. Although the incident made the news, the *Genoa Weekly Courier* calmly reported: "the wagon ran off the grade, causing quite a smash-up." The following year, teamster Louis Lenwick was bringing a load of shingles down Kingsbury grade from Hobart with a four-horse team when he hit an icy spot at the "first bridge above the Farmers' Mill." Luckily, Louis got off with just a broken rib and a dunking in the creek.

Albert Bohlman grading Kingsbury's dirt surface in the 1930s, using an official Douglas County grader. (Photo courtesy of Dale Bohlman).

Then in May, 1892, someone made the bad decision to continue tugging an engine up Kingsbury Grade with a 12-horse team during a heavy snowstorm. The engine was destined for use at a logging camp near Meyers, but wound up being dumped off onto its side when the wagon's wheels "dropped into a hole that was covered with snow." The team and driver came out alright, but the engine later had to be rescued.

And now the <u>best</u> part: recollections from our readers of old Kingsbury Grade "back in the day." Because there's nothing quite like the voice of experience!

> "My mom said they made movies on that road. I remember the hairpin turn punctuated by the lone pine tree."

> "I can remember traveling up the grade, scared to death that my father would get close to the edge on a sharp turn with a corduroy surface, and we'd all go over the edge! And

I remember how relieved we were to make it to the 'piped' spring [where we could] refill the boiled-out radiator."

"Many of the young men (my brother and my husband among them) who belonged to Carson Valley's 20-30 Club would go up to the Lake after their meeting, and they'd talk about coming home in the early morning via Kingsbury with the sun in their eyes."

"The lookout point was constructed by the local Kiwanis Club, I think. It became more of a 'necking stop' than an actual scenic look-out."

"When I was in high school, the road was still dirt and people from California driving Kingsbury Grade would hug the side that is against the mountain and you would have to go around them on the wrong side because they were scared to go near the edge."

"I remember in winter they would close the road with just a couple of sawhorses and a board. If the snow was not too deep we would just move the sawhorses aside and just use it anyway."

Chapter 1 - Landmarks/Places

We've never found an actual photo of Peters Station. But other writers have speculated it may have looked something like Friday's Station, shown in this Lawrence & Houseworth photo circa 1866. The freight wagons that stopped at Peters Station would certainly have been similar to these.

PETERS STATION ON OLD KINGSBURY

Halfway up Kingsbury Grade once stood an early hotel known as Peters Station. If you were a teamster, this was the place to stop!

Situated on a flat spot at a big bend in the trail, Peters Station was a welcome oasis where men and animals alike could eat, drink, and rest from their labors ferrying goods up and down the dusty track.

Not all the teamsters who stopped here would cram into Peters' three-story hotel to sleep at night, of course. Many were content to simply roll up in their blankets in the bed of their wagons or stretch out on the ground. At one time, the hotel was said to employ five

Chinese cooks and five waitresses, and as many as 300 wagons could be found tied up at Peters Flat overnight. And it wasn't just teamsters who stopped at Peters Station, of course. Travelers headed east or west would have paused here for water. The Pony Express, too, paid quick visits during its brief period of operation over Kingsbury Grade from spring 1860 through October, 1861.

So just who was the "Peters" of Peters Station? Born in Virginia in 1804, Richard Peters had been a mule-skinner himself before morphing into a station owner. Richard, his wife, Elizabeth Elvira (Enlow), and their seven children had crossed the plains in 1850 at the height of the Gold Rush, settling initially in Fremont, Yolo County. Perhaps lured by fresh mining strikes, the Peters family moved on to Grass Valley in 1851.

About 1860 the Peters family moved once again. This time they picked a small spot located about halfway down the fresh Kingsbury Toll Road to set down their roots, a site that soon became known as Peters Flat.

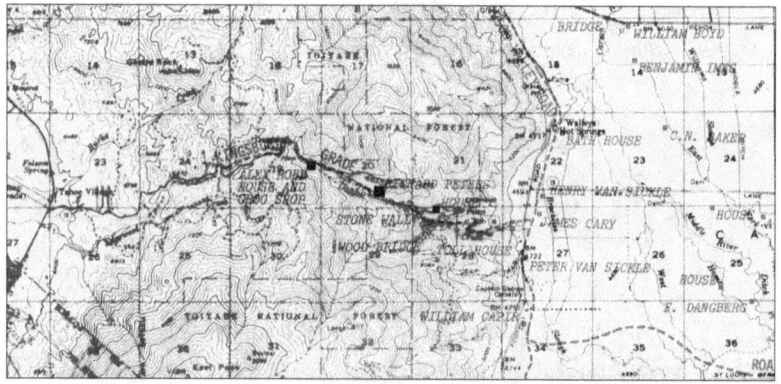

This reproduction of Lt. Ives' 1861 map shows not only the home of Richard Peters but also Alex Robb's "house and grog shop" slightly farther west, and a third house to the east. (Reproduction map courtesy of Douglas County Historical Soc. & Museum).

The ground here was relatively level and timber abundant. Nearby springs afforded them water. The family planted a garden in a meadow close by and raised staples like corn, beans, potatoes, beets and tomatoes for the hotel's table. Although perched at an elevation of 6,400 feet, their gardening efforts proved a splendid success. The

Chapter 1 - Landmarks/Places

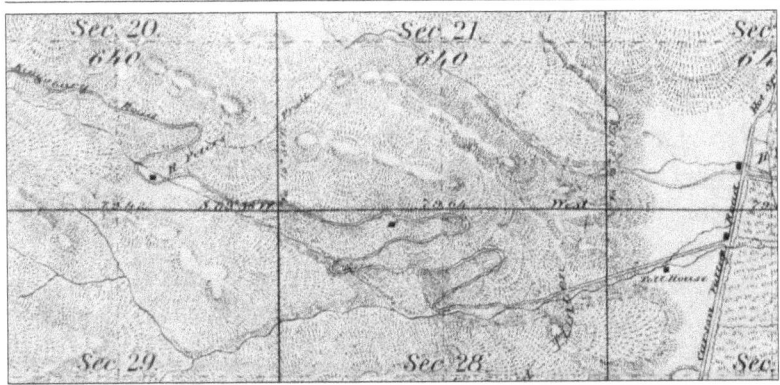

Ives' 1861 survey map shows R. Peters' waystation tucked in a big bend of the Kingsbury road (near top left).

family would later claim that their vegetables ripened two weeks before crops in Carson Valley.

Richard Peters' timing for launching his new station was auspicious – and probably not coincidental. Kingsbury & McDonald officially opened their new wagon road in August, 1860 (and it actually was in use several months earlier). The new toll road quickly become the preferred route for teamsters hauling goods to Genoa or Virginia City, not only shortening the distance but also cutting travel time from Placerville to Carson Valley by a full day.

But the early Kingsbury dirt roadway was steep and difficult to navigate. A pause to rest at the halfway point made perfect sense. Other settlers began to appear about the same time along this downward stretch, too. By 1861, a "grog shop" was in full swing just west of Peters' Station, while yet another settler had built a house a bit farther down the canyon.

Young Richard M. Peters, the eldest son of the family, had been born in Missouri in November, 1839. That made him about 21 years old when the family first opened their station, and he soon began to cast his eye around for a wife. Options for a marriage mate must have been slim pickings indeed at the Peters outpost on the side of a mountain. But not far away was Lake Tahoe and the growing settlement at South Lake.

On September 22, 1863, wedding bells were ringing. Richard M. Peters and Miss Frances Marion Lapham, a Tahoe girl, tied the knot right there at the Peters family hotel. Richard was not quite 24 years old at the time; Frances was a mere 14. Despite her youth, Frances would have been no stranger to the hard work of running a hotel. She was the daughter of "Capt. Billie" (William W.) Lapham, a former hotel proprietor himself at Calaveras Big Trees and, more recently, a hotel and commercial fishing boat operator at South Lake Tahoe. Frances and Richard would go on to have nine children together.

Wedding certificate for R.M. Peters and his wife, Frances M. Lapham, married September 22, 1863 at Peters Station. Richard's sister, Clara, was a witness. (Courtesy Douglas Co. Historical Society).

But patriarch Richard Peters did not get to enjoy his new station for long. He died there at Peters Flat on February 19, 1866. It was "the dead of winter," and the roadway would have been covered in snow. Somehow, his body was ferried up Kingsbury Grade and buried "at Rowland's Station in Lake Valley" (now known as the Pioneer Cemetery at Al Tahoe). Peters was 61 years old. His wife, Elizabeth, would live on for another 25 years, finally passing away in Ely, Nevada on December 17, 1891.

After his father passed away, Richard M. and other members of the family continued to run Peters' Station for a time. Timber was abundant and, according to family lore, they added logging to supplement their hotel income. In later years a sawmill was said to be

The grave of family patriarch Richard Peters at Al Tahoe. (Born in Virginia, Dec. 2, 1804; died at Peters Flat, Feb. 19, 1866.)

Chapter 1 - Landmarks/Places

operating at Peters Flat. One brief newspaper mention confirms that as late as 1892, two trips a day were still being made from Peters Station to Hobart using horse-drawn teams to haul cedar posts.

Eventually, however, Richard M. sold Peters Station (some say it was bought by Peter Van Sickle), and moved away. Family history says he went on to try his hand at mining in Ward, Nevada (south of Ely) and other sites in Central Nevada. He died on June 6, 1915 in San Francisco, and is buried at Cypress Lawn Cemetery.

The hotel itself is long gone, though as late as the 1980s a few surviving fruit trees still marked the site of Peters Station. Today, the spot where Richard Peters and his family once welcomed hundreds of teamsters is part of the Humboldt-Toiyabe National Forest.

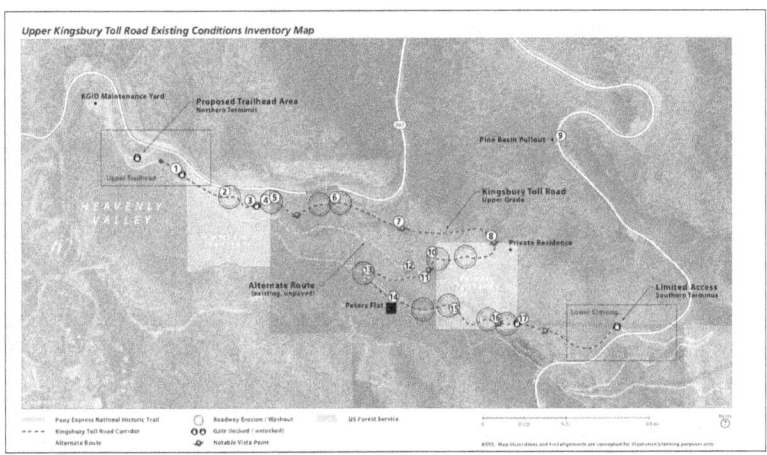

U.S. Forest Service map showing the winding white line of present-day Kingsbury; dashed black line for the old Kingsbury Toll Road; and Peters' Flat (small black square).

Family information for this story comes from materials kindly contributed by Dr. Perry Close (a Peters family descendant) to the Van Sickle Research Room at Douglas County Historical Society & Museum about 1992. Many thanks to DCHS for the marriage certificate and first map shown above. Special thanks are also due to historian Sue Silver for her wonderful input, research and encouragement for this article, and especially for sharing the 1861 Ives map.

Downtown Minden, Circa 1918. (Photos on this page courtesy of Douglas County Historical Society & Museum).

SO MANY MINDENS

The photo above gives a glimpse of the early commercial district of Minden, Nevada about 1918, roughly a dozen years after its 1905 debut. Business was booming as you can see by the crush of cars, including that svelte roadster at right.

The upstart "Minden Creamery" (as it sometimes was casually called) was launched in 1908 at 1620 Water Street, and by mid-1914 had put its older competitor, the un-electrified Carson Valley Creamery, out of business.

The new Minden butter facility actually had a longer and fancier formal name: officially, it was the "Minden Butter Manufacturing Company." Principals in this new creamery enterprise included H.F. Dangberg, Jr. — the same luminary behind the creation of Minden itself — William Dressler,

The new Minden Creamery, about the time it opened.

Chapter 1 - Landmarks/Places

Fritz Schacht, and Richard Fricke. With John Sattler as its first butter-maker, some said the new creamery produced the "finest butter in the West."

Privately-held when the organization first began, Minden Butter Mfg. eventually morphed into the Minden Co-Op Creamery in 1946. The creamery's doors finally closed in 1961, however. Time stands still for no man, woman, or dairy!

But as for the "Minden Creamery" token shown to the right, helpful research by dedicated token collectors confirms that *this* token came from a different creamery altogether — in Minden, Nebraska!

A creamery token from a different "Minden"!

What a fascinating coincidence: two creameries with similar names operating at roughly the same time, in two different widely-separated towns, both called Minden!

All of which got us to pondering: just how many Mindens *are* there? The short answer: at least *seven* here in the United States alone!

There's a southern Minden, touting its location "in the piney woods of northwest Louisiana," founded in 1836 by a lawyer who later ran off to California during the Gold Rush.

There's rural Minden, Texas, named by a homesick former Louisianan, who somehow found himself in Texas about 1849 and affixed the name of his hometown (that same "piney woods" one) to a spot in need of a name along an early Texas stagecoach line.

A bit farther north, Minden, Iowa sprang up beside the Chicago, Rock Island and Pacific Railroad and the imagination-tickling "Keg Creek." Settled by German immigrants, this Minden is said to have been named for the former hometown of many of its "industrious settlers."

Minden, New York, formed in 1798, similarly took its name from its namesake town in Germany. This New York settlement once was touted as a "gateway to the west," thanks to its prime location ad-

Forgotten Tales:

joining both a railroad and the Erie Canal. Today the town covers nearly 33,000 acres and is divided into six smaller hamlets, one charmingly named "Mindenville."

Not to be left out of the mix: Minden, West Virginia, named (once again) for old Minden, Germany; it's said that the name was picked by an early West Virginia coal-mining official. Sadly, the spot is now a Superfund clean-up site, with nearly a third of its residents said to suffer from some type of cancer. It was annexed into the neighboring city of Oak Hill in 2015, but remains on the books as a "census-designated place."

And then there's our creamery-twin Minden, Nebraska — home of the token that prompted this virtual journey. Originally a plot of empty land "without a single inhabitant or building," this town of Minden was voted into existence in 1876 by nearby homesteaders, stripping county seat-hood from railroad-dominated Lowell to the north by their vigorous exercise of democracy.

Our very own Minden, Nevada got its name from H.F. Dangberg, Jr., who envisioned a well-ordered community surrounding a town square (today's grassy Minden Park), and named it (of course) after the old German town near his father's birthplace.

If these widely-scattered Mindens begin to sound like a road trip in the making, one couple has already blazed the way! A great story was carried by the *Record-Courier* about Terri and Chuck Luettgerodt of Minden, Nevada, who set out in a Volkswagen van in 2017 to visit "every Minden they could."

Minden, Nevada got its name from H.F. Dangberg, Jr., the dapper gent shown in this early-1900s photo.

Chapter 1 - Landmarks/Places

Special thanks to noted Nevada historian and long-time token collector Michael Fischer and token experts Jack Haddock and Leroy Felch for their kind help in identifying the origin of the Nebraska "Minden Creamery" token and their kind suggestions for this story!

Like to learn about the "other" Mindens? Here are some links where you can read more about them!

Minden, Louisiana: *http://www.mindenusa.com/*

Minden, Texas: *http://tinyurl.com/y2y6ss88*

Minden, Iowa: *http://mindeniowa.com/History.html*

Minden, N.Y.: *http://townofminden.org/town-history/*

Minden, West Virginia: *https://en.wikipedia.org/wiki/Minden,_West_Virginia*

Minden, Nebraska: *http://www.mindennebraska.org/*

Forgotten Tales:

Main Street, Gardnerville, looking north, in the 1920s.

THE GRAND RITCHFORD HOTEL

William Ritchford was bound and determined to be a hotel owner. In March, 1893 he purchased the Gardnerville Hotel at the southwest corner of Main and Eddy Streets from Hans C. Jepsen. Here at his "fine hotel and saloon," the accommodating new owner offered board and lodging by the day, week, or month. Patrons of his saloon were promised not only "good wines, liquors and cigars," but also an opportunity to try their luck at the card tables.

Ritchford had a partner in this new endeavor, Hans Nelson. And for a time, things went swimmingly. In June of 1893, the pair were already planning to build an addition to their hotel to "accommodate the transient custom that nightly make this a stopping point," said the *Genoa Weekly Courier*. But by March of 1894, Ritchford had sold out his interest to Nelson for a bit more than $5,000, and was moving to Antelope Valley with his family.

Chapter 1 - Landmarks/Places

They weren't gone long, however. By October of 1896, the Ritchfords were back in Gardnerville, renting the lower floor of Pete Wilder's house. By 1897, Bill Ritchford was operating a livery and feed business in town. But he still had heart set on another hotel.

About 1898, Ritchford purchased a parcel on the west side of today's "S"-curve, then the south end of Gardnerville. An early blacksmith shop occupied the south corner of the property (opened by Chris Nelson and later operated by Fred Fricke). By March that same year, carpenters and stone masons were hard at work erecting a new hotel for Ritchford at the north end of his property.

Things didn't get off to a terribly auspicious start. First, carpenter Henry Beste took a nasty fall at the under-construction hotel, confining him to bed rest for a day or two. Then the following week stone mason Henry Mathews, who'd been hired to lay the building's foundation, suddenly passed away.

But by mid-July, Ritchford and his family were able to move into their new hotel. The building was finished enough that the newspaper was able to report on its "imposing appearance," with a cornice painted a patriotic red, white and blue. In November, 1898 Ritchford added a tall water tank to the property, bringing gravity-fed water to the new building. Genuine "horsepower" of the old-fashioned kind was used to lift the large tank into place.

The Ritchford Hotel circa 1900, with its prominent water tower. Below, advertisement for the "Grand House Warming" when the hotel opened in 1898.

That September, 1898, a "Grand House Warming" celebration and dance was advertised to celebrate the new hotel. In deference to the size of the expected crowd, festivities were held just up the street at Valhalla Hall. Tickets for the event cost $2, but thoughtfully included not only supper for attendees but also "horse feed."

Even so, however, it appears the new hotel building was not quite finished. In June the following year, the *Courier* reported plans under way to "immediately finish" the third story of the hotel, "owing to the throng of people in Gardnerville." A Sanborn Fire Insurance map drawn that year shows a two-and-a-half story "boarding house" on the property. Ritchford finally had his own hotel.

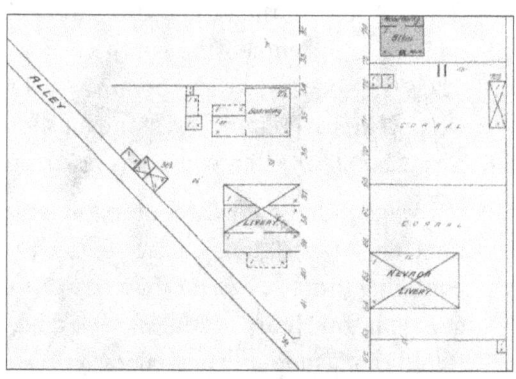

Sanborn Fire Insurance Map from 1899, showing a 2-1/2 story "boarding house" and a livery stable to the south.

Advertisements in the *Genoa Courier* in late 1899 cheerfully informed the traveling public that Ritchford's new hotel was open for business. He had picked an auspicious official name for it, too: "The Latest." Guests could stable their horses at the livery just 38 feet to the south (possibly a new incarnation of the former blacksmith shop).

And Ritchford wasn't done yet. By early 1900, carpenter Henry Dixon was "finishing up" what may have been more of the third story of the Ritchford. When finally completed, the Ritchford Hotel featured 20 "first-class" rooms. Mrs. Ritchford charmed guests with her cooking,

"THE LATEST."

Under the above name, Wm. Ritchford's new hotel is open to the public in Gardnerville.

Superior accommodations in board and lodging. Transient custom given special attention.

Livery and Feed Stable

In connection. Careful attention given to transient custom and freight teams.

Fine Turnouts, Reasonable Prices.

Both hotel and livery are up-to-date.

WM. RITCHFORD, Prop.

Ad for "The Latest" in Genoa Weekly Courier, 1899.

Chapter 1 - Landmarks/Places

including "sumptuous" turkey dinners. The livery business did so well that in 1902 a "large addition" was made to the stable. And in 1903, in keeping with the hotel's name "The Latest," Ritchford had his hotel electrified — a significant improvement over the original gas lighting.

"Word of the Ritchford Hotel spread around the state, and anyone traveling through the valley wanted to stay there," noted Scott Schrantz in his 2006 blog, *Around Carson*. "Even in San Francisco they spoke of its elegance and luxury."

And more improvements were yet to come. In the fall of 1905, Bill Ritchford added an "ice house" to the hotel and a "rustic front" to his stable. This latter change, the *Record-Courier* noted approvingly, "greatly add[ed] to [the stable's] appearance." By 1907, Sanborn maps show that another narrow addition had been made to the livery stable, pushing the building even farther south. And by 1912, almost the entire southern corner of the property had been covered with various extensions to the livery building.

Ritchford worked hard to ensure a steady stream of patrons to his hotel. After the V&T opened its Minden depot in 1906, Ritchford drove his team to meet the train every day to pick up "drummers" (traveling salesmen) needing a place to spend the night.

Among other amenities for guests, medical help was close at hand for anyone who needed it. As early as 1899, a patient was said to be "undergoing treatment at Ritchford's hotel." Advertisements from 1908 indicate that Dr. E.H. Hawkins kept both his medical office and his residence in the hotel. Another physican named Dr. Marotz had a convenient office nearby, and "at night [he] can be found at [a] cottage adjoining Ritchford hotel," according to Marotz's ad.

But at the age of 75, after more than two decades in the hotel business, Bill Ritchford passed away in a tragic accident. It was February of 1922. Despite his years, Ritchford was hauling hay from Minden to Gardnerville on a sled with a four-horse team. The load of hay slid forward, spooking the horses. Ritchford fell off and was dragged for several hundred feet. The sled ran over his body, and his chest was crushed. Ritchford died the following day.

Son Bill Ritchford, Jr. continued to carry on the hotel business for the next two years. But not long after Bill Sr.'s death, his wife's health began to fail. Anna passed away in August, 1924, and was buried beside Bill in Carson City's Lone Mountain Cemetery.

A few months after his mother's passing, son Bill, Jr. sold the old Ritchford Hotel to the Aja family. It was still quite a place, featuring "stove heat," electric lights, a parlor, two offices, a soft drink concession, dining room and kitchen, according to a 1923 Sanborn map. With automobiles having usurped the place of horses, the former livery stable had by now been converted to a painting shop and "temporary fire headquarters."

What remains of the Ritchford Hotel today. Gone are the third story, the front porch and architectural embellishments, but the bare bones of the old hotel still remain.

The former Livery stable, after innumerable additions.

Today, a portion of the gracious three-story Ritchford Hotel still stands. The current wooden structure is now just two stories tall, thanks to a fire that broke out on the third floor in January, 1937. Although the lower floors were saved, the top floor of the hotel was never rebuilt.

Chapter 1 - Landmarks/Places

Next time you pass by, remember the tall water tower that once stood beside the Ritchford, boosted into place using old-fashioned horse-power. Think of the many smiling guests who crossed its threshold to enjoy Bill's hospitality and Anna's home-cooked dinners. And imagine Gardnerville's early days, when the gracious Ritchford Hotel was known as far away as San Francisco.

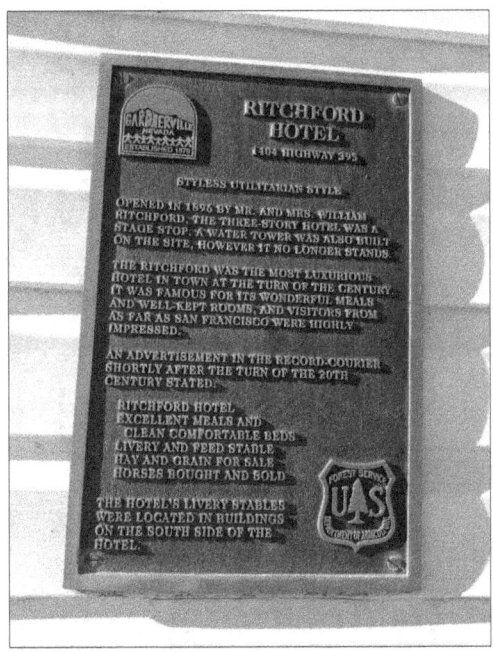

Historic plaque commemorating the much-beloved, long-lived Ritchford Hotel. This plaque notes the hotel was first opened in 1896. (Our research suggests his hotel actually opened in 1898.)

THE GARDNERVILLE BRANCH JAIL

If it isn't *the* ugliest jail structure west of the Mississippi, the Gardnerville Branch Jail probably ranks among the top ten. Its walls are poured concrete; its lower door is metal; and the boxy shape is (as one writer so politely put it) "devoid of architectural detail or ornamentation." Inside, the jail saved space by giving prisoners the penitential equivalent of Murphy beds: fold-down steel bed frames, attached to the wall.

Douglas County shelled out just $25 for Louis Springmeyer to draw up the plans in 1910 (and some might argue *that* was too generous.) But believe it or not, the Gardnerville Branch Jail holds a coveted position on the National Register of Historic Places. And

Chapter 1 - Landmarks/Places

there's a perfectly fabulous story filled with politics, positioning and power behind how this tiny small-town jail came to be built!

Segue back in time to the year 1910, when Genoa was the official county seat and boasted the only county jail. Roads were primitive and automobiles were few, but crime was an equal opportunity occupation. So although Gardnerville had its own share of criminals, it had no hoosegow of its own in which to conveniently house them.

L.S. Ezell, East Fork Justice Court judge since 1884, had come up with a makeshift solution: he kindly allowed constables to use his Gardnerville granary building to lock up offenders whenever needed. This may have been convenient for the law enforcement officers, but it wasn't such a grand idea from the prisoners' point of view. The local newspaper called the granary a "vile hole" and "no fit place for a human being."

East Fork Justice of the Peace L.S. Ezell (his middle name was "Socrates," a great name for a judge!)

Opportunity for a better solution knocked when Judge Ezell finally retired in 1909 after some 25 years on the bench, and thoughtfully donated his granary property to the county. Local citizens petitioned the commissioners to build a new and improved branch jail in its stead.

It seemed like a grand plan. But politics is a tricky thing. Eager for the new town of Minden not to be left behind in the dust, H.F. Dangberg, Jr. launched a *counter*-petition, protesting against building the jail in Minden's competitor, Gardnerville. When the County commissioners formally took up the issue in April, 1910, local heavyweights William Dressler and H. Park joined with Dangberg in the protest.

As government officials so often do, the beleaguered commissioners listened politely — and went right ahead with their original plans. Approval was given to build a one-story jail in Gardnerville. And as government officials *also* frequently do, they soon *expanded* the project to make it two stories, adding a courtroom on the top floor.

Now that there was to be a new branch jail, an official branch jailer would also be required. Albert Daudel was hired for the post, at $2 per day — upped to $4 for more arduous days when he'd oversee a chain gang fixing county roads.

Although Genoa wasn't eager to relinquish its time-honored post as the official county seat, Fate had other ideas. On June 28, 1910, much of Genoa was destroyed by fire — a loss that included the County's main jail and courthouse. Luckily, only one prisoner was being housed in Genoa's jail at the time. The weather was warm and the new Gardnerville jail was, thankfully, already under way. The prisoner was simply "chained to a post" until he could be moved to the still-under-construction branch jail in Gardnerville.

Within just a few more years, Minden succeeded in wresting away the crown of official county seat. And by 1916, a brand new County courthouse was erected in town, which included jail cells in the courthouse basement.

Officially, all county prisoners were now *supposed* to be incarcerated at Minden and, officially, the Gardnerville branch jail was discontinued. But for reasons of economy, convenience, habit, or perhaps lingering tensions between the two towns, Gardnerville's old branch jail continued to be used for prisoners well into the 1950s.

As the National Register listing diplomatically expressed it in 2003, the old Gardnerville jail remains "an excellent example of turn-of-the-century jail architecture," with its steel cages, large hasps and padlocks, bullpen and woodstove all still intact.

Those poured-concrete, steel-reinforced walls may be plenty ugly. But they certainly were practical; they successfully kept Gardnerville's prisoners "from digging through the barriers as they had in Genoa's brick jail."

It's not a museum — yet, although some say plans for that re-use are under way. So there's no way to stroll the inside, peer out the

Chapter 1 - Landmarks/Places

upper courtroom's windows, or check out the fold-down metal beds. But you *can* check out the exterior of this turn-of-the-century jail for yourself at 1440 Courthouse Street, Gardnerville, Nevada. And if you do, be sure to look for the plaque.

The Gardnerville Branch Jail is listed on both the National and Nevada State Registers of Historic Places.

Forgotten Tales:

Portions of the original horizontal siding are beginning to peek out from beneath the later-added vertical layer. Look carefully at the windows flanking the front door and you can still see the outlines of the original pair of doors.

THE EAST FORK SCHOOL

Once, this humble little building was the pride of East Fork.

As early as 1876, a small schoolhouse was already serving pupils in the East Fork School District, south of Gardnerville. Parents were so unhappy with the school's original location, however, that a vote was held that year to compel its removal to "a more central" spot.

Back then, folks thought nothing of dismantling an entire building and then hammering back together again somewhere else.

Notice of moving the school to a "more central" location. (Carson Valley News, October 6, 1876).

Chapter 1 - Landmarks/Places

Soon, the early East Fork school had been spirited off to its new and improved location. Now sitting just north of Wheeler's Twelve Mile House (today's Smoke Shop) and three miles south of Gardnerville, the reconstructed school was perched on the east side of the river, across from the Wilslef home. No bridges crossed the river there, however. "In the spring when the water was high, there wasn't much school," chuckled Peter Wilslef in an interview with the *Record-Courier* in 1958.

But just moving the old building to this new location wasn't enough for the ambitious school district. By July 1880, bids were being solicited to construct a spanking *new* school building. Miss Emma Jennison, the East Fork teacher in those days, must have been heartily pleased with her fresh classroom. As for the old, original school building, it wasn't forgotten as a potential revenue source; the empty shell was auctioned off to the highest bidder in December, 1880. Waste not, want not.

The school's new organ, manufactured by Chappell & Co., may have looked something like this.

Local parents aspired to make East Fork School the "best schoolhouse in the county, outside of Genoa." So after the new building was up, additional improvements quickly followed. New desks were purchased for the pupils in 1882, and a "fine Chapel organ" was added in 1884. Somewhere along the line, the school acquired a warm and welcoming school bell, too.

The school building served as a meeting place for the whole East Fork community. Sunday services were held inside its walls for decades. And when voting time rolled around, the schoolhouse was turned into a polling place. On Christmas Eve, 1884, the entire East Fork community gathered there around a communal Christmas tree to exchange presents and greet Henry Beste, all dressed up as Santa.

Enterprising teachers pulled together "programmes" for the enjoyment of the community, with students as the entertainment. Fidgeting youngsters would recite carefully-memorized pieces and sing off-key but chipper songs. Much to the delight of parents, sometimes those memorized tunes were even sung in German. Fees for admission to these gala events (50 cents a head) went toward purchasing new books for the school's library.

Teachers were a precious commodity, and not just for the book-learning they dispensed. Marriage-age female teachers, often from other towns, could be important additions to the local gene pool. One teacher followed the other at the East Fork School in rapid succession, typically leaving when either a husband or a better position was found. Following Miss Emma Jennison behind the teacher's desk in the classroom were Julia McCord, Ida Pettegrew, Kate Nevin, and May Tierney. Miss Hattie Cushing, one of the longest-lasting East Fork schoolmarms, taught there from September 1893 through 1902 before moving on to teach at Mono Lake.

Competition among districts to snag the best teachers could be intense. Miss Eugenia Arnot, daughter of Alpine County judge N.D. Arnot, was lured away from her post at the Gardnerville School in July, 1902 with a can't-refuse offer of $70 per month to teach at East Fork – a twenty-five percent increase over what she previously had been making.

Mary Eugenia Arnot in her graduation picture from UNR, 1900. (Courtesy of descendant M. Shively).

In its hey-day, East Fork School attendance ranged from roughly twenty to forty students. Those who learned their 'Three R's' within its walls reads a bit like a "Who's Who" of old Carson Valley: Allerman, Bartels, Berning, Frantzen, Hussman, Dangberg, Jacobsen, Robishaw, Rodenbah, Settelmeyer, Springmeyer, Syll. Kids arrived

Chapter 1 - Landmarks/Places

Inside the East Fork schoolroom about 1898. Gathered atop the teacher's raised platform are teacher Harriet Cushing (top right) with students (from upper left): Emma Hussman (who later married Wm. Nelson); Jennie Jacobsen (Mrs. George Fay); center: Sue Rodenbah (Mrs. Bert Selkirk). At bottom are Minnie Jacobsen (Smith) and Bertha Dangberg (who married Joe Cardinal). (Photo courtesy of Douglas County Historical Society & Museum).

in carts and aboard wagons, on horseback, and by foot. But by 1915, the East Fork School had outlived its usefulness. Its twin doors (one for boys, one for girls) were closed for good.

Such a sturdy wooden building couldn't go to waste, however. Henry Elges bought the structure and moved it near the "S" bend in Gardnerville, to become Elges' "green goods and vegetable store." Elges was followed by John and Norma Ellis, who briefly operated their own grocery store there.

By the mid-1930s it had become the Gardnerville Laundry, operated by George Oka before being acquired in

Advertisement for the Nishikida laundry, Record-Courier, December 31, 1959.

August, 1940 by the Nishikida family, which continued to own the establishment for over 25 years.

Today, almost no one gives this humble wooden building a second glance. But next time you drive by, we hope you'll remember its past. Not so very long ago, it was the pride of East Fork parents, the cheerful roof under which a community once gathered. Listen carefully and maybe, just maybe, you'll catch the faint echo of a welcoming school bell.

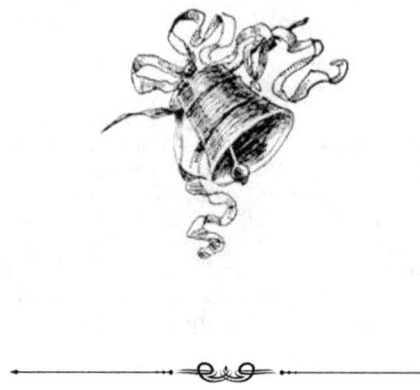

Chapter 1 - Landmarks/Places

The <u>second</u> Fairview School building, circa 1908. (Photo courtesy of Douglas County Historical Society & Museum).

FAIRVIEW SCHOOL

We still don't know exactly when the *first* Fairview schoolhouse was built. But it had to be sometime before 1875 – because that's the year its teacher, Mrs. Ella S. Layne, became the "Heroine of Fairview School District"! And a well-deserved honor it was.

The early Fairview School occupied a spot at the mouth of Fay-Luther Canyon. And like most buildings of the era, it featured a handy woodstove to help ward off the chill of winter. Teachers' duties often included arriving early to light the stove before their students arrived.

All was well until one chilly day when, in the midst of her lesson, Mrs. Layne happened to glance up. Quickly changing plans, she seated herself at the school's organ and commenced a rousing rendition of "Onward Christian Soldiers." This was the students' cue to march outside for a recess. No one (except the teacher) realized that the loft had caught fire from the woodstove's chimney until the children all had made it safely outside the burning building. A heroine she was, indeed!

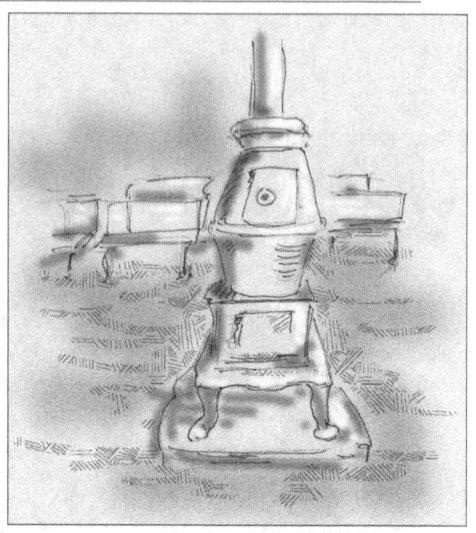

A wood-fired pot-bellied stove was a central feature in many a one-room schoolhouse.

A few more tidbits about the early days of the Fairview School have been handed down to us courtesy of old-timer Owen E. Jones, who set pen to paper in 1925 to record his recollections. Fairview was the "first schoolhouse built in [this end of] Carson Valley," Jones assures us. The very first teacher? A Mr. Spencer. And the school itself moved around a bit; the first one initially sat at the mouth of the canyon, about a mile "west" [probably northwest] of the spot where a second incarnation of the school later stood.

A public building like a school was, after all, a public building; so the community embraced the Fairview schoolhouse for other local needs as well. Following its weekday service as a one-room school, the building donned a new role on Sundays as a place to hold church. Separation of church and state? No one bothered their heads about such things, back in the day.

And there's a hilarious story about one of those religious gatherings in the Fairview School, again preserved for us courtesy of Owen E. Jones. It seems that Abednego Johns, a pioneer Jacks Valley rancher, had arranged for two distinguished LDS ministers to come and preach there one Sunday in late October, sometime in the 1880s. Mr. Johns, his wife, and the two visiting ministers – all "heavy-weighted persons" – clambered aboard his wagon and rode

Chapter 1 - Landmarks/Places

happily south for the event. The Fairview schoolhouse was filled with local neighbors, eagerly awaiting the out-of-town preachers. And then Mr. Johns stood up to introduce his guests.

Now, Mr. Johns was a "very splendid old gentleman," Owen Jones tells us, whose "only fault was that, when he got to talking religion, he never knew when to stop." So after his introduction of the two visiting Mormon ministers commenced, Mr. Johns just kept on talking! By the time he finally ceded the floor, most of the assembled crowd had given up and left the building. The two preachers were forced to simply dismiss the stragglers and call it a night.

Advertisement for a typical farm wagon in 1876.

And that, as it turns out, wasn't entirely the end of Mr. Johns' rather unfortunate evening, either. While his "fillibuster" wound on, some wag had decided to play a Halloween joke. Slipping outside, the prankster swapped the front and back wheels of Johns' wagon, then added a heavy sack of wet sand beneath the driver's seat and tied another to the rear axle. When the non-preaching event finally was over, Johns and his guests boarded the wagon only to endure an excruciatingly slow journey home in the dark. They were mystified about why their team was so incredibly exhausted – until they finally reached Jacks Valley and discovered the prank.

As we've mentioned, the first Fairview School originally sat at the mouth of Fay-Luther canyon. But roughly twenty years later, a new and improved, second Fairview school was built about a mile to the south. Was this just a more convenient site? Or were there other reasons for starting over?

That question's a mystery. But we do know that well-known local builder John Cress was chosen as the contractor, and the new schoolhouse quickly sprouted at the corner of today's Fairview and

Fredericksburg Roads in the summer of 1893. When school began again that fall, the teacher at the new one-room school was a Miss Lloyd. Just imagine how she must have enjoyed moving into the freshly-built quarters!

Could this the first day of school at the new, <u>second</u> Fairview School building, in the fall of 1893? It seems a good bet! There are no trees visible around the schoolhouse (those arrived in 1894). If so, that may be Miss Lloyd in back right, with her 24 students. This rare photo is on exhibit at Douglas County Historical Society, with a child's antique alphabet-block just visible at lower left. (Photo courtesy of Judy Wickwire).

The following spring, Miss Lloyd had a grand idea for beautifying the grounds. In honor of Arbor Day, 1894 (the last Friday in April), Miss Lloyd put her students to work planting trees around their new schoolhouse. Then each student took on the responsibility of watering the tree they had planted.

"We hope the trees will live and flourish," enthused the *Genoa Weekly Courier* on April 27, 1894, "and that the teacher and pupils will be able to enjoy their shade for many years." That happy wish that would come true – and not just for Miss Lloyd's helpful students, but for generations of Carson Valley residents to come. Several of those early saplings still adorn the site today!

Chapter 1 - Landmarks/Places

A further upgrade arrived in January, 1901, when Allen & Dake bored a new well to serve the school. Its fortuitous location in the bottomlands made this a relatively easy task; the new well only needed to go 40 feet deep. It probably helped greatly with keeping those trees watered. And how many thirsty students must have paused to get a drink from the school's handy new "pump well"?!

The number of pupils attending Fairview School seems to have stayed fairly constant, at least for a time: 29 students were in attendance in 1881, and 25 occupied its desks in 1901. But Fairview was said to have been one of the roughest posts for teachers. "The Dresslers and the Bohlmans and the Ruhenstroths were all tough boys," recalled one long-time Valley resident. "They would put skunks in the girls' billy [the outhouse]. So the teacher made the boys use the girls' outhouse!"

Perhaps those rowdy kids help explain why Fairview teachers seemed to come and go with great rapidity. Mr. Spencer, the school's first educator, was replaced by Mrs. Layne in 1876. By 1883 Katie Taylor had taken over, only to be replaced by Miss Belle Leslie in 1888 and Mrs. Mary Field in 1889. None other than Ellen Virgin (daughter of the Genoa judge) was engaged to teach at Fairview for the term beginning fall 1890. The tree-planting Miss Lloyd stuck it out for a few terms from 1894 to 1897 before returning to her home in Empire. The year 1898 featured a Miss Lamb from Washoe County as the teacher, while Nellie M. Cavanaugh was in charge for the 1899 and 1900 terms before departing to take the post of principal at the Oak Grove School in Santa Clara County, California. In 1904 the Fairview School District secured their next teacher, J. Novacovich, from Reno. And that's not an exhaustive list; there were likely a few other teachers as well!

But it's hard to fight progress. As with many small school districts, economics eventually forced the tiny Fairview School to close. Fairview's School District was merged with Minden's School District in the spring of 1929. The old Fairview schoolhouse was auctioned off that same year, with Charles Mapes becoming the successful bidder. About 1939 the old building was moved up the road to the Crosby Ranch (later Ahern Ranch), where some say it was converted to a bunkhouse and others say it became an office. Today, as far as we know, all traces of the old school seem to be gone; local researchers say they have tried to locate it, without success.

But those amazing Arbor Day trees planted by the students and their thoughtful teacher back in April, 1894? By the time the photo at the top of this chapter was taken circa 1908, the tiny saplings were mature trees. And some of them are now giants!

These graceful survivors have continued to offer shade and shelter for 125 years – and still counting. Miss Lloyd must be smiling indeed.

Original site of the Fairview School, looking south, with its 125-year-old trees. A private residence now occupies this parcel. (Rick Dustman photo).

Chapter 1 - Landmarks/Places

Three Reasons to Visit the Old Genoa Cemetery (Besides Snowshoe Thompson)

The most famous inhabitant of the Old Genoa Cemetery is Snowshoe Thompson – whose grave is visited so often there are special signs that point the way!

But here are three *more* reasons you might want to pay a visit to the Genoa Cemetery next time you're in town:

(1) It's Beautiful.
From gorgeous spring flowers to the gentle deer that make it home, this peaceful graveyard is just plain beautiful. You'll want to admire the vintage details on ornate metal fences and elaborately carved headstones. Winter or summer, there's always something special to see here – and beautiful things to record. So be sure to bring your camera!

Spring daffodils. (Judy Wickwire photo)

(2) It's History.

The welcoming arch over the Old Genoa Cemetery's entrance dates it to 1865, and the very first burials here might be even older.

They say a town's history can be found in its graveyard, and that's ever-so-true here in Genoa. A stroll through this old cemetery is a great way to get acquainted with the early history of Carson Valley – sometimes dubbed "Cousin Valley" for the close relationships linking pioneering families!

Here you can find the monument for David Walley, founder of Walley's Hot Springs. A proud black pillar (said to have been brought all the way from France) commemorates the Adams family, whose kiln provided the brick for many early buildings in Genoa and Carson City. And keep your eye out for "Fiddler" Carl Taylor's headstone, a gifted musician who used to play at weddings and dances all over the Valley in the 1880s (when he wasn't too tipsy to play!) It's all part of the history of this fascinating area.

(3) It's Fun Solving Mysteries.

Not every grave at Genoa Cemetery is identified – sometimes only tiny clues remain! Many of its original wooden headstones were burned by a well-intentioned "clean-up crew" during the Great Depression. A few wooden markers have survived, however, and cemetery officials have helpfully added markers for unidentified graves.

Wooden marker for J.R. Johnson. (Judy Wickwire photo).

Just recently, an old newspaper article allowed cemetery officials to identify four unmarked burials in a plot ringed by eight granite pillars. And old photos, oral histories, letters and other information could identify more "unknowns" in the future. You can help, simply by putting the word out. We never know whose attic might contain additional helpful information!

Chapter 1 - Landmarks/Places

CROSSING THE RANGE ON SNOW SKATES

SNOWSHOE THOMPSON'S HEADSTONE STOLEN?!

Well, *almost!* Here's the fascinating tale of how Snowshoe's grave at Genoa Cemetery got capped with concrete — and who's sleeping in the long-forgotten grave next to him.

Snowshoe Thompson, you may remember, exited this life on May 15, 1876 at his ranch in Diamond Valley, California. Just 49 years old, this giant of a man is said to have been felled by an opponent he couldn't fight: a burst appendix.

It took nine long years before Snowshoe's widow, Agnes, was able to have a tombstone placed on his grave. But when she finally did, the headstone was a thing of beauty. Carved of white marble, it features a carved pair of miniature skis, crossed in silent mourning.

John A. "Snowshoe" Thompson, as he looked about 1870.

But though Snowshoe's grave was now properly marked, it became something of a mess. Agnes died in 1915, and Snowshoe's only son passed away just two years after his father. With no one left to care for the family plot, the brush and weeds began taking over.

Until Decoration Day, 1924, that is. (Never heard of Decoration Day? A predecessor of Memorial Day, Decoration Day was started to honor the Civil War dead, and was expanded after World War I to include those killed while serving in *any* war.)

On that fateful 1924 Decoration Day, a thoughtful little girl from Gardnerville decided Snowshoe's grave deserved a champion. A "self-appointed guardian angel," she pulled the weeds and laid flowers on Snowshoe's nearly-forgotten grave that year — and for years to come. Even though Snowshoe hadn't died in a war, she felt he merited that special remembrance.

Erected by Snowshoe's widow in 1885, Thompson's headstone features a pair of crossed skis. The Thompson family plot is now neatly protected by a concrete cap — paid for by funds raised by Genoa school children. (Rick Dustman photo).

Years passed, and eventually other school children took up the cause. Hearing that "persons unknown" had callously attempted to steal Snowshoe's headstone (unsuccessfully, thank goodness!), children in Genoa began raising funds to anchor his stone firmly in concrete.

Thanks to their efforts, by the end of May, 1948 (now known as Memorial Day), the Thompson family plot had been covered over in two feet of heavy concrete. (They were taking no chances!) Public-spirited Genoans Carl Falcke, Sr., Arnold Juchtzer, and Joe Gossi pitched in to do the heavy labor.

Chapter 1 - Landmarks/Places

And so Thompson's headstone was happily safeguarded from thieves, and the family plot protected from encroaching sagebrush. It's a great tale of community involvement and local generosity. Once unkempt, Snowshoe's grave is now such a point of pride that special signs mark the way for eager pilgrims.

Next time you pay a visit to Snowshoe's marble marker, take a brief look around for the long-forgotten grave of John Sauquet next door. Today, nobody even knows Sauquet's name. But back in Snowshoe's time, Sauquet was a "honcho" in tiny Alpine County.

Born in France about 1818, John Sauquet was well over forty when he made his way to the mining boomtown of Silver Mountain City. He opened a general merchandise store there about 1865, selling groceries, provisions, mining supplies — and, of course, wines! (He was, after all, a Frenchman!) Sauquet did so well that between 1865 and 1870 the value of his inventory jumped from $800 to $2,000 — not an easy feat, in a town where mining busts typically followed the short booms.

John Sauquet's grave near Snowshoe's, in Genoa Cemetery. The weeping willow is a symbol of mourning. (Rick Dustman photo).

Sauquet tried his own hand at mining speculation, becoming a trustee (director) of the Mountain Mine. And when mining entrepreneur Lewis Chalmers racked up an unpaid bill approaching $4,000, Sauquet took title to the Imperial Silver Quarries mine as a way to satisfy his judgment.

By February, 1881, however, Sauquet (now in his early 60s) had become ill. He ventured as far as San Francisco to consult a doctor, and in October, 1883, left Silver Mountain behind entirely, moving his merchandise from the now nearly-abandoned town to the tiny settlement just below it at Silver Creek. Sauquet hung on two more years, finally passing away September 27, 1885.

Here's the fascinating connection to Snowshoe Thompson: Sauquet drew his last breath in Diamond Valley at the home of Agnes Thompson Scossa. Snowshoe's widow and her new husband, John Scossa, took care of Sauquet in his final illness. As a token of his gratitude, Sauquet's will left everything he owned to John Scossa, assets that included real property in San Francisco as well as in Alpine. All those old Alpiners knew each other. And Snowshoe Thompson — though he's buried in Genoa — was an Alpiner, too.

And a short P.S. - Look closely at Snowshoe's headstone. The "P" in Thompson is missing! Exactly why remains a mystery. But some say either Agnes or John Scossa may have accidentally given that misspelling to the stone-carver.

The crossed skis on Snowshoe's headstone commemorate his many years as the "mailman of the Sierra." (Rick Dustman photo).

Agnes Singleton Thompson Scossa is buried next to her first husband, Snowshoe Thompson. (Rick Dustman photo).

Chapter 2

RANCHERS & LOCAL FOLK

John Q. and Ellen Adams.

THE ADAMS RANCH

Today, the historic Adams ranch home is nearly hidden from the highway among century-old trees. It's just a mile north of Genoa. But few people know the early house is even there, or how deep the family's legacy runs in Carson Valley.

The two original Adams brothers, Rufus and John Q. Adams, left Adams County, Illinois with their father and arrived at Salt Lake, Utah, in May, 1850. The Adams boys brought with them an important skill they'd learned back home: the art of brick-making.

After three years in Utah, the brothers decided to push even farther west together. Perhaps they'd been bitten by the gold bug; they tried their hand at mining for a time at Placerville, California, according to family lore.

If so, gold riches apparently eluded them. The pair arrived in Carson Valley on June 1, 1853, a time when the largely-unsettled area was still part of Utah Territory. Here the brothers purchased a large tract of land north of Mormon Station. They not only began farming and raising cattle, but finding good-quality clay on their property, opened a brick yard as well. Their early training served them well!

Artist's rendering of the two-story brick Adams home in 1881, with its nearby orchards and cattle.

At first, the brothers built a small wooden residence. A few years later, however, they sold half of their land and, with the funds, constructed an imposing two-story brick home. The new Adams home was made of bricks fired on the property in the brothers' own kilns.

For roughly its first five years, the gracious 22-room home became part-residence and part-business, serving the ocean of eager travelers passing by its front door along the Emigrant Trail. Functioning as a way-station, it not only offered lodging to travelers but also hay and barley for their animals. Amenities included the usual bar where thirsty travelers could find a drink and also separate parlors for men and women. Upstairs, a grand ballroom provided a welcome spot to hold local dances.

The Adams brothers were wildly successful, and not just as a result of their welcoming home or fertile fields. Adams brick was soon in great demand, and became a popular building material as settlements grew in Carson Valley. Bricks from the Adams brickyard were used when the Genoa Courthouse was erected in 1865 (with Rufus Adams himself as one of the two building contractors). Adams brick also was said to be used in the U.S. Mint in Carson City, and as far away as Virginia City.

Rufus, the older of the two Adams brothers, never married. He died at age 48 of heart disease in 1876. His health had been poor for several years, and when he'd written his will in California the previous year, he acknowledged that "I am liable to die at any time."

Adams brick was used in many early buildings in Carson Valley, and may well have been used for this Genoa structure, built as a store by J.S. Childs in 1862.

Younger brother, John Quincy Adams, continued to work the ranch. He had a help-meet in his endeavors; he'd married Canadian Ellen Dolan in Virginia City on October 1, 1866. By 1881, the family's assets had grown to include a 820-acre farm, valued at $12,000. The couple also had three children: Mary Lydia (born July 18, 1867), John Elias (born December 24, 1868), and William Rufus (born November 16, 1871).

John Quincy Adams lived to see the 1800s give way to a new century. He died suddenly in 1910 at his home in Reno, at 78 years of age. Wife Ellen followed him in death another 11 years later (in 1921), after a protracted illness. She was 84.

While all three of the Adams children were successful, eldest daughter Lydia had perhaps the most surprising career. Born in 1867, she attended the State Normal School in San Jose, California and then Stanford University in Palo Alto, California, studying to become a teacher. If she was hoping for a position close to home after graduation, luck was with her. The principal of the Genoa School fell ill, and Lydia was appointed in April, 1890 to fill his position as school principal. She was just 22 years old.

That same year, Lydia married local newspaperman Delbert E. Williams, owner/editor of the *Genoa Courier*. At almost 40 years old Williams was nearly twice Lydia's age, and had only recently re-

Chapter 2 - Ranchers & Local Folk

turned from a stint in Hawaii in an effort to regain his health. Nevertheless, he and Lydia were married in Carson City on Thanksgiving Day (November 27, 1890). Over the next few years Lydia would help him compile an extensive genealogy of the Williams family, but their marriage ultimately did not prove successful. They divorced in 1898.

In 1904, the now-single Lydia moved to Washington, D.C. to teach school. But she still had a passion for adventure. In 1906, when Walker Lake Indian Reservation was opened for mining, Lydia returned to Nevada to "join the rush." Driving a horse and wagon "on a hard run . . . in the wild race for rich mineral lands in Dutch Creek (Mineral County, Nevada)," she became the first female locator in that new mining district.

Polished, educated, and adventuresome, Lydia Adams-Williams never forgot her roots in rural Nevada.

She returned again to Washington, this time employed by the Department of Agriculture to "spread the gospel of the desert": writing and lecturing about the benefits of irrigation and resource conservation in the West. Through this position she became friends with both President Roosevelt and President Taft, and was a frequent visitor at the White House.

Lydia tried her own hand at politics in 1921-22, running for the post of Nevada State Senator. She traveled all over Nevada to connect with voters, walking, hitching rides, and at one point even getting a lift from a circus to reach her destinations. But her campaign for state senate was unsuccessful.

Following several years of poor health, Lydia died in Los Angeles, California in 1929, at the age of 61. She is buried with her pioneering relatives in the Adams family plot at Genoa Cemetery.

The shiny black Adams pillar is one of the most prominent monuments in Genoa Cemetery, and is said to have been brought all the way from Europe. Different faces bear the names of family members. Top image shows the names of Lydia's brother, William, and his wife Katie. The names of Rufus W. Adams (John's grandson) and wife Elsie are shown at right. (Top photo by Rick Dustman; photo at right by Judy Wickwire).

Chapter 2 - Ranchers & Local Folk

It Wasn't Always Called Jubilee Ranch

The iconic old barn on Foothill Road has "Jubilee Ranch" emblazoned on the side. If you're like me, you've driven by it hundreds of times. And if you're *also* like me, every time you've gone by, you wished you knew its tale! So, who built this great old barn, and when? And what's the backstory to the name "Jubilee"? We did a bit of digging — here's the story!

Yes, it turns out, it's an old-old ranch — one of the very first ranch claims in Carson Valley. Some sources suggest this ranch was originally owned by settler John Cary in the early 1850s. Sometime after Cary, the property was acquired by soon-to-be Senator J.W. Haines and was known as the "Old Haines Ranch." And around 1857 (even before the Comstock Lode boomed), Haines sold the ranch to Peter Van Sickle.

Henry Van Sickle.

Born in New Jersey, Peter was the younger brother of Henry Van Sickle. And Henry, as you'll recall, was the early pioneer who ran the famous "Van Sickle Station" hotel and stage stop just up the road.

Peter, like his brother, was considered a "thrifty Dutchman" and he, like Henry, was skilled as a blacksmith. In addition to this prosperous hay and dairy ranch (620 acres of it, by 1881!), Peter also operated a blacksmith shop in Genoa at the northwest corner of Main and Nixon Street. Peter and his wife, Lillies, lived in a small house near the church just up the street from his blacksmith shop.

Lillies and Peter Van Sickle.

Peter eventually grew tired the blacksmith trade; in 1888 he placed an ad in the paper, trying to sell his shop and other holdings. It seems he wasn't successful at finding a buyer, however; in 1892, his Genoa blacksmith shop had been leased out to W.J. Armstrong, another blacksmith.

As for the giant barn at his ranch south of town, Peter is said to have built the current structure about 1900. It's a giant indeed: some 65 x 100 feet in size. Built using a "peg-and-groove" technique, Peter's barn resembles that of his brother Henry Van Sickle's barn up the street. Unlike Henry's barn, however, Peter's lacks windows.

W. J. ARMSTRONG

Has leased P. W. Van Sickle's Blacksmith shop in Genoa and is prepared to do

Wagon & Carriage Work

AND

Repairing of Agricultural Implements of all kinds.

TIRE SETTING $4 AND UPWARDS.

HORSESHOEING A SPECIALTY.

Armstrong's ad in the Genoa Weekly Courier, *February 19, 1892.*

The lower floor of the Jubilee barn was once used for dairy cows, and loose hay was stored in its 13,000-sq.ft. second-floor loft. Although today the Jubilee Ranch barn appears to be all on a single level, some say it was originally built into the hillside (a style called

Chapter 2 - Ranchers & Local Folk

"bank-a-hill"), so hay could be loaded into the hayloft without requiring a hoist. (It could also be that this actually describes Henry Van Sickle's red barn slightly farther to the north, which clearly follows the descending contour of the hillside).

Henry's red barn, slightly farther north, tucked into the hillside, shown from the downhill side.

In addition to his dairy ranch, Peter Van Sickle was also in the meat business, and by 1883 was running two meat wagons to supply local demand. Not all Peter Van Sickle's customers were happy ones, however. Alpine mining mogul Lewis Chalmers wrote Peter a snippy letter in 1879, complaining: "The beef you are now sending me is not of the same quality as you sent me at first, and not such as I intend to pay for."

An early view of Henry Van Sickle's barn, viewed from the uphill side. Note the windows.

Leander Hawkins, too, had unhappy memories of working for Peter Van Sickle at the tender age of 10. When Leander requested the heifer that had been promised to him after a full year's work, Van Sickle reportedly refused to deliver it.

Still, Van Sickle had his generous side as well. In 1895, Peter and Lillies adopted a little two-year-old boy whose mother had died.

They renamed him Oscar Van Sickle and Oscar became part of the Van Sickle family, along with their own four children.

Peter Van Sickle passed away in 1908, at the age of 77. He and Lillies had just celebrated their 50th wedding anniversary the previous year. Adopted son Oscar continued to run the Peter Van Sickle Ranch until 1927 when it was sold to Thomas Summers, becoming known as the "Summers Ranch."

In 1951, a young entrepreneur named Ted Bacon bought the ranch. At the time, Summers was using the ranch to raise pigs. Rather than rename it after himself as the "Bacon Ranch" (which would have been pretty funny for a hog farm), Ted chose a name reflecting a recent trip he had taken to England, when a "jubilee" had been held to celebrate the crowning of the queen. The "Jubilee Ranch," he said, was a "happy name."

And there you have it — the fascinating story of this historic ranch, and how it got its "Jubilee" name!

The graves of Peter and Lillies Van Sickle at Mottsville Cemetery.

Chapter 2 - Ranchers & Local Folk

Photo of the Ferris Ranch by Juanita Schubert, circa late-1930s. (Courtesy of Douglas County Historical Society & Museum).

FERRIS RANCH

Just one lonely image, captured by Juanita Schubert in the 1940s. That was all that was left of the old Ferris House. Or so we thought.

But wait! Locals informed us the old Ferris home still exists in Carson Valley – it was just relocated in the 1940s, and now sits off Stockyard Road, a few miles east of its original location. So, naturally, we went "off on the hunt" to find it.

Back in its day, the house stood in a fairly remote location, about four miles east of Genoa and at the crossroads of two early roads. From the west, the Boyd Toll Road meandered in from Genoa before heading southeast across the valley. And from the north, the Cradlebaugh Road headed down the valley from Carson City and continued on south.

In terms of today's geography, that translates into north of Muller Lane, on the west side of Hwy 395. And there's a great landmark that can help you find the right spot today: the old house once sat just below the prominent Douglas County "D" on the side of the hill. (Look closely at the photo above, and you can make out the white "D"!)

The Ferris family arrived in Carson Valley in September, 1864, after crossing the plains by wagon train from Galesburg, Illinois – George W.G. Ferris, his wife Martha, and eight of their ten children. (Son Fred was a soldier in the Civil War at the time; and daughter Harriet had died as a baby in 1849).

This actually wasn't the first trip west for George Ferris, Sr.; back in 1851 he'd spent seven months in California seeking Gold Rush riches with relative Chauncey Noteware.

George Washington Gale Ferris, Sr., circa 1889. (Photo courtesy of Dangberg Home Ranch Historic Park).

Although Noteware remained in the west (later becoming Nevada's first Secretary of State), Ferris had quickly realized there were more lucrative opportunities for him at home, and returned to Galesburg. But he never stopped dreaming of returning. And so in 1864, George Ferris and his family finally made the long, hard overland haul by wagon, heading (they originally thought) for San Jose.

Perhaps it was sheer economics that led Ferris to abandon San Jose as a destination and determine to settle in Carson Valley instead. Perhaps the beautiful scenery won him over. Or perhaps relative Chauncey Noteware (by then living in Carson City) had some hand in the decision. However it happened, once here, the Ferrises decided to stay.

Back in Illinois, George Ferris, Sr. had been a well-to-do farmer. He realized a handsome sum by selling his Illinois farm – some say as much as $60,000. But he had taken his profits in greenbacks. To his dismay, he found that here in Carson Valley, greenbacks were disfavored and he was forced to pay for his new land in gold. He

Chapter 2 - Ranchers & Local Folk

would later tell listeners that he'd lost $10,000 to $12,000 by the conversion. Descendants told an even worse tale, saying he'd realized a mere *fifty cents* on each greenback dollar.

Ferris promptly set about building a home, and by 1865 the family had what one biographer called a "rudimentary ranch house" in Carson Valley. Great-granddaughter Grace Dangberg would later describe the home as constructed "with nails hammered out on the anvils of Henry Van Sickle." The plaster on its interior walls was mixed with horsehair for strength, she tells us (a common building technique at the time). And the parlor featured a fancy fireplace with a marble face. Not quite so "rudimentary," after all!

Daughter Margaret Gale Ferris, who married H.F. Dangberg. This photo is circa 1880s. (Courtesy of Dangberg Home Ranch Historic Park).

In years to come, the Ferris house would be the scene of many happy memories – and several tragic ones, as well. One of the happiest events took place in March, 1866, when Margaret Gale Ferris (daughter of George Ferris, Sr. and older sister of Ferris Wheel inventor G.W.G. Ferris, Jr.) married prominent rancher H.F. Dangberg, here in her family home. She was just 17, while Dangberg was in his middle-30s – twice her age. Margaret lived thereafter on the Dangberg Home Ranch, and raised her children there.

Although the house would continue to be referred to as "the Ferris house" for many years, the family actually didn't live here for long. In 1868, George Ferris, Sr. purchased a nearly-new home in Carson City from Gregory A. Sears. The "Sears-Ferris House" had just been built in 1863, and it still stands today at 311 West Third Street.

The Sears-Ferris House in Carson City, at 311 West Third Street.

Just why the Ferris family left Carson Valley and moved to Carson City is a matter of some dispute. One story has it that the family feared the local Washoe Indians after an accidental shooting raised hard feelings. But as historian Richard G. Weingardt put it, George Sr. was simply "tired of living on an isolated ranch." Carson City probably offered a more citified existence and greater social and cultural activities for the well-heeled family.

Whatever the precipitating reason, in 1868, just four years after arriving in Nevada, the Ferris family moved to Carson City. There George Sr. continued his passion for farming as a "gentleman farmer." And he did his best to beautify his new hometown; it's Ferris who is credited with planting hickory, black walnuts and chestnut trees on the grounds of Nevada's Capitol building. He would eventually sell the Sears-Ferris House in Carson to his daughter, Mary, in 1890.

As for the Ferris Ranch in Carson Valley, Grace Dangberg tells us that the family eventually sold it to Margaret's husband, H.F. Dangberg, who leased it to tenant farmers. So over the coming decades, the Ferris house didn't stay empty.

And here's where the tale turns tragic. German immigrants Anna and Fritz Sarman arrived with their family in May, 1882, and took up residence in the former Ferris house. The Sarman family continued to live peacefully in the home for the next dozen years. Then on May 8, 1895, Anna was brutally murdered inside the house – struck in the head with a hatchet.

Suspicions focused at first on Anna's husband, Fritz, who claimed to have been out in the fields at the time. But he and other supporters contended the culprit must have been a passing tramp. It was true that drifters along the nearby roads would often stop in at the house for a meal, and one had just eaten breakfast there the day Anna was killed. Sadly, Anna's murder remains a mystery that's never been solved.

The Ferris house would become the scene of yet another sad event some eight years later, in 1903, while newlyweds Henry and Viola Berning were living in the old Ferris home. The young couple had just tied the knot on Christmas Day, 1902 in Gardnerville. Young

Chapter 2 - Ranchers & Local Folk

Viola soon found herself pregnant with triplets – a nearly unheard-of medical event for the day. About October 17, 1903, Viola successfully gave birth to three tiny girls: Nina, Ina, and Mina. Baby Nina died shortly after birth. And just nine days later, mother Viola, too, died here at the Ferris house (October 26, 1903).

The old Ferris house no longer stands in the fields where Juanita Schubert snapped its picture. But traces of the former occupants still turn up occasionally near the site. An early dime, a silver-plated pocket watch, and parts from various agricultural implements have been found over the years.

View toward the site where the Ferris home once stood, with the old fence line still in place. (Rick Dustman photo).

And where did everyone go? Mother Viola Berning and baby Nina are both buried (although in unmarked graves) at Genoa Cemetery. Viola's remaining two triplets, however, lived on into their 70s. George Ferris, Sr. moved to Riverside, California in 1881, dying there in April, 1895. George Ferris, Jr. died in Pittsburgh, PA in 1896, at the entirely-too-young age of 37. Fritz Sarman passed away in May, 1900, almost exactly five years to the day after his wife's murder. Margaret Ferris Dangberg passed away in 1946 and rests at Lone Mountain Cemetery.

As for the old Ferris house itself, it was moved to the sheep camp on Stockyard Road about 1942. A subsequent owner had the house significantly remodeled, and used it as a second home when he and his wife came down from Reno. In recent years the old house became part of the Bently holdings and has served as a ranch manager's home.

So this wonderful piece of history is still here, square nails and all! For all the tragedies this old house has seen, how lovely to know it's still a survivor.

The Ferris house, as it looks today, on Stockyard Road in Minden. (Rick Dustman photo).

Chapter 2 - Ranchers & Local Folk

Courtesy of Dangberg Home Ranch Historic Park.

DANGBERG RANCH

Where's that "Wayback" machine when you need it?! It's hard to be rock-solid certain you've separated fact from fiction after more than 160 years have passed. But if there was one person in the world who had good reason to hate Lucky Bill Thorington, it was probably Heinrich Friedrich ("Fred") Dangberg. And some would hint that he eventually got his revenge.

Dangberg was born September 16, 1830 in Halle, a province of Westphalia. Although today we know it as Germany, it was officially the Kingdom of Prussia at the time. Fred's father was a farmer and stage operator. But Fred, the oldest of four sons, didn't follow in his father's footsteps immediately. Instead he was apprenticed to an uncle to learn the trade of operating a flour mill.

In 1845, when Fred Dangberg was just 15, his father passed away. His mother would remarry two years later, in 1847. All together, this added up to a rough period in the young teen's life. His relationship with his step-father was not a happy one and, with war looming in Europe, he faced the very real possibility of being conscripted.

Young and ambitious, Fred Dangberg was in no mood to wait for Fate to overtake him. In 1848, at the age of 18, he sailed from Germany to New Orleans. Lying ahead were not only fresh opportunities but a life on his own.

In America, Dangberg initially found a job rafting logs down the Mississippi. The following year, Dangberg and a friend, Benjamin Mast, followed the river upstream to St. Louis, where they secured work in a flour mill. And in 1850, the pair hired out as farmhands at a ranch in Illinois.

Fred Dangberg circa 1880. (Courtesy of Dangberg Home Ranch Historic Park).

In the meantime, of course, the Gold Rush had begun. The lure of riches and land proved too compelling for ambitious young men like Dangberg and Mast to ignore. In the spring of 1853, the pair left St. Louis and headed west, driving 200 head of cows and oxen with them. They reached Gold Canyon on October 11, 1853, and promptly set to work panning gold.

For the next two-and-a-half years they would split their time between mining and trading, running their sluice box in the months when water was available, and trading goods to emigrants when water was scarce. They purchased wares in Placerville and Sacramento, and sold everthing from flour, coffee and similar staples to simple comforts like tobacco and alcohol.

By early 1856 Dangberg had branched out into the dairy business, too, and began selling butter – more than 450 pounds of it that year alone, counting the weight of the small wooden barrels (firkins) that held it. He decided to abandon gold mining entirely and turn his energies to ranching instead.

Sometime that same year (1856), Dangberg settled on 320 acres of rich bottomland beside the East Fork of the Carson River, land that

Chapter 2 - Ranchers & Local Folk

would later become known as the Klauber Ranch. Dangberg began building a log cabin, and set his cattle to grazing nearby. But as far as we can tell from recorded documents, Dangberg never bothered to file a formal land claim. Maybe he was working on it. Maybe he intended to hire a surveyor, and just wanted to get his cabin up first.

But Dangberg, it seems, wasn't the only one with an eye on that same stretch of land. Returning home from a supply trip over the mountains, Dangberg found local trader and land baron Lucky Bill Thorington occupying his partly-finished cabin – armed with a gun and backed up by a group of supporters. Some say Lucky Bill taunted Dangberg, boldly declaring that he'd jumped Dangberg's land claim and demanding "What are you going to do now, Dutchman?"

Although this may well have been Dangberg's take on the situation, entitlement under early land claims was a far more nuanced matter. An intervening 160-plus years makes it doubly difficult to tell for sure, of course. But here's one fascinating tidbit that might help explain the confrontation: these 320 acres *might* be the same property that had been claimed and surveyed by Fred Heath and F.D. Clift on August 9, 1856.

Assuming it's the same land, the big question of course: did the Heath/Clift survey happen before or after Dangberg settled on the property? Did Dangberg perhaps even buy out Heath and Clift's interest in an unrecorded transaction? Or did he begin building his cabin, unaware of their claim? On the other hand, could *Lucky Bill* have bought the Heath/Clift land claim? Or might Lucky Bill have been friendly with Heath and Clift, and just trying to help pitch out what they felt was an intruder? We may simply never learn the truth. But it's possible that Lucky Bill – a resident of Carson Valley since 1853 – honestly believed that he or his friends had a valid right to the land.

By the time Dangberg arrived, would-be settlers were swarming into Carson Valley and land disputes with those who'd settled earlier were common. Newcomers frequently had difficulty finding unoccupied land and many bitterly resented those who'd arrived before them, believing it unfair that early settlers had tied up such huge swaths of land.

It would seem out-of-character for Lucky Bill to have taken advantage of a newcomer, especially by force. He was apparently well-liked by many (though not all) in the community, with contemporaries describing him as a "merry citizen." Tales are still told of his kindness toward unfortunate travelers.

Lucky Bill certainly had no need to steal land, having already amassed a home in Genoa, an extensive ranch in Eagle Valley, and another ranch at Fredericksburg. On the other hand, Lucky Bill was a strong enough personality he probably wouldn't take it lightly if he felt that someone was trying to take advantage. So perhaps the dispute was simply an unfortunate collision between two determined individuals, both believing they were right.

"Lucky Bill" Thorington was a local trader and land baron. (K. Dustman illustration).

The confrontation was certainly an unequal one. Fred Dangberg was a strapping young man, and hard work had made him strong. But Lucky Bill, topping six feet, was even larger. Worse yet for Dangberg, Lucky Bill had friends standing by his side.

Finding himself substantially outnumbered – and perhaps also aware that his own unperfected claim might be somewhat shaky – Dangberg abandoned his partly-finished cabin and sought out other land to claim. He moved south about a mile, crossing the river and heading upstream. There, in 1857, Dangberg and partners Ben Mast and C.E. Holbrook took up 640 acres of land in the middle of the fertile Carson Valley – land that ultimately would form the nucleus of the Dangberg Home Ranch.

From a water-rights perspective, it was a canny move. Here where the East Fork and the Middle Fork separated, Dangberg had first ac-

Chapter 2 - Ranchers & Local Folk

cess to the water that flowed on to downstream ranchers – including Lucky Bill. And, this time, the partners made sure they did things right: they hired a surveyor and set out corner markers for their property.

But the earlier confrontation with Lucky Bill Thorington was one that Fred Dangberg never forgot – and likely never forgave. When Thorington was hauled up on trial in June, 1858 for his alleged complicity with murderer William Edwards, eighteen jurors were plucked from the community to hear the charge. Old-timers including Thomas Knott and Harry Hawkins would later hint that Dangberg was a member of that jury. Others, however, dismiss such an allegation as pure rumor.

Rumor or not, perhaps no one was happier than Fred Dangberg on June 19, 1858 when Lucky Bill was dispatched into eternity by a hangman's noose. Some two years after the confrontation at the cabin, Dangberg might well have felt Lucky Bill had finally gotten his come-uppance.

And oh yes. There was one final celebration ahead for Fred Dangberg: he finally, *finally* was able to purchase the Klauber Ranch in 1902!

Beautiful and just a touch mysterious, this is what the Thran House looks like today.

TALE OF THE THRAN HOUSE & AN OLD TRUNK

I'm going to build you a grand house in Carson Valley, like we have in Germany!" promised Dietrich Thran.

And a grand house Thran built for his wife, indeed! Completed about 1910 to 1911, the house featured stained glass over the front door, stately pillars out front, and a gigantic room upstairs for dancing.

Thran was born in Germany July 15, 1864, and arrived in Carson Valley when he was 17 years old. He applied for naturalization, becoming an American citizen in October, 1886. After working for

Chapter 2 - Ranchers & Local Folk

other ranchers and saving his pennies, at age 30 Thran was ready to find himself a wife. In late 1894, Thran returned to the Old Country and in May, 1895, came back to Carson Valley — bringing with him seven other Germans, one of whom was his new a fianceé!

Marie Dieckhoff, Dietrich's intended, was all of 16 years old. They wasted no time — just one month after Marie set foot in Carson Valley, she and Dietrich were saying their "I do's." They were married on Saturday, June 29, 1895 at the home of Herman Thran, Dietrich's brother. Dietrich presented her with a beautiful horse and buggy all her own as a wedding gift. (He really knew how to charm a gal!)

Dietrich (known locally as "Dick") rented the Tucke Ranch that summer, and he and a friend purchased an expensive California thresher together. Just one year later, Dick became a dad for the first time: little Emma Thran joined the family on November 2, 1896. Baby Richard followed a year later, in December, 1897.

Dick continued to do well financially, and by fall, 1897, he had purchased the 160-acre Marsh Ranch for $6,000, at the corner of today's Highway 88 and Dressler Lane. The Thrans took possession of their new ranch the following spring.

Though the acreage was large, their living accommodations were anything but. Dick, Marie, and their growing family moved into a house so small that today it is used as a tractor shed. And "growing" their family was: their third child, Carl, arrived in September 1899, and little Mariechen (who would grow up to marry Chris Cordes) followed two years later, in 1901.

The Thran family and their four children originally lived in this small building — today a tractor shed.

In 1908, Dick had a large barn constructed on his ranch (by noted barn-builder Henry Hanke, it's believed), complete with concrete floor for the milking side. But the Thran family continued to reside in the small shed-like structure. (Ranching priorities, you know!)

Finally, in April, 1910, the Thran family went back to Germany for a four-month visit. Seeing the large and beautiful German homes, Dick promised his wife, Marie, he would build a similar home for her in Carson Valley. And true to his word, he did! Their graceful two-story home on Dressler Lane was constructed about 1911 (possibly also by Hanke).

The barn was built in 1908, probably by noted barn-builder Henry Hanke — before the family residence was constructed. (Judy Wickwire photo).

The original stained glass panel remains over the front door of the Thran House. (Judy Wickwire photo).

The Thrans' dairy operation continued to thrive. Eventually the family was milking some 65 cows. They also raised pigs and chickens, and sold eggs. The shed the family had lived in for over ten years was converted to a house for the separators, and later, a chicken coop.

Dick Thran passed away in 1937 and Marie in 1946, and the family home was passed down to their three boys. Son Carl never married, and continued to live in the house all his life. After Carl's death in 1980, the property was purchased by Jack and Maria Martin, who still live there today. But oh, the deferred maintenance they discovered when they took over!

"When I first walked through the old house, I cried," said Maria. "I said, 'We're living here?'" The beautiful front columns were rotted and infested with bees. The roof was so decayed blue sky showed

Chapter 2 - Ranchers & Local Folk

through. And inside, walls were soot-covered from the coal-burning stove. "One of the workers was out on the balcony and put his foot through the balcony floor," recalls Maria.

The large upstairs room once used for dances was cluttered with — well, stuff. "Over the years, when they had something they didn't know what to do with, they just put it upstairs," explains Maria.

But one special treasure was discovered in the original old shed. All dirty and greasy, it was a steamer trunk, filled with old auto parts. Maria rescued it from the trash pile and made sure it was saved, cleaned and refurbished.

It just *might* be the same trunk that accompanied 16-year-old Marie Dieckhoff all the way from Germany to her new life in America.

The old trunk has now been lovingly restored. (Photo courtesy of Judy Wickwire).

Roy with his mother, Marie Thran, circa summer 1926, in the front yard of their home. (Photo courtesy of the family.)

THE LEGACY OF ROY THRAN: A BOY & A BOX

A ten-year-old boy. A small box of his most prized possessions. And over 80 years later — a very special legacy shared.

Born June 10, 1925, Roy Thran was the last of five surviving children of Dick and Marie Thran. (You may remember our earlier story about the beautiful Thran House.) Roy's mother, Marie was 48 years old when he was born, and had already lost three other intervening children. So Roy's arrival must have been a time of great rejoicing. He was christened in the Lutheran Church on Sunday, June 21, 1925.

Roy did his lessons on a slate at the Minden School. He caught butterflies, played with metal trucks, dabbled with paints, and enjoyed games of marbles and Tiddledy Winks with friends. Someone

Chapter 2 - Ranchers & Local Folk

(perhaps his father) carved him his very own wooden baseball bat. No doubt Roy had chores to do at the family's dairy ranch on Dressler Lane. And even as a ten-year-old, he kept a stained and much-battered stuffed toy he'd carried in his toddler days.

Smitten with the great aviators of the day, Roy joined the Jimmy Allen Flying Club for kids, receiving an official acceptance letter, a silver pilot's bracelet, and a bronze pin with "flying cadet" wings. Roy even owned his own pint-sized version of the aviator cap worn by Charles Lindbergh on his history-making solo across the Atlantic in 1927.

Father Dietrich (Dick) Thran, daughter Mariechen, and youngest child Roy, in front of the Thran house on Dressler Lane circa 1927. (Photo courtesy of the family.)

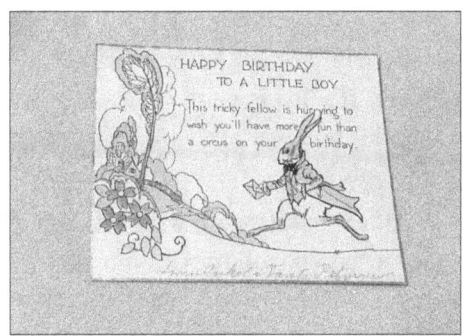

Roy's birthday card, from "Onkel & Tanta Behrman."

Roy celebrated his tenth birthday that summer of 1935. His beloved Tante Behrman, his mother's sister, wished him "more fun than a circus" in a cheerful birthday card.

But according to a story handed down through the family, Roy's mother, Marie, had an awful premonition. As she glanced at Roy one day, chilling words formed across his forehead: "I won't be here long." And not long after the vision, Roy's family was attending his funeral at the same Lutheran Church where he'd been christened.

On August 6, Roy had gone to visit a childhood chum. They took a leisurely ride on a horse, and grabbed a late lunch, and decided to take a dip in the West Fork in the late afternoon. They rode out to a spot by a dam near the Schwake Ranch. The water was deep, and neither boy could swim. Roy stepped off the bank into the cool water — and disappeared.

Roy's young friend rode quickly for help. But by the time Roy's body was recovered, it was too late. Two doctors tried in vain for several hours to revive him.

Imagine Marie's grief: her premonition had come true. Carefully, she packed away all of Roy's treasures: his aviator cap, his school books, his slingshot, his birthday card. A butterfly pressed in the leaves of a book. It all was gently tucked in a special box, handed down through the family for more than 80 years.

Roy Thran in his school picture from Minden School, October, 1931. (Courtesy of Douglas County Historical Society & Museum).

And then in 2019, with the family's permission, Roy's treasures were shared with the community in a very special exhibit at the Carson Valley Museum. Two glass cases were devoted to displaying the loves of a ten-year-old boy growing up in 1935, preserved just as he left them. An amazing snapshot in time.

"So many people were touched with sadness back then, and now this journey will come full-circle," notes Krista Jenkins, a Thran descendant. "The sadness will be different now. Memories have softened with the passing of time, and it's nice to know that this journey of the 'Boy In A Box' will now be told again to a different generation."

Special thanks to Krista Jenkins and the Thran and Cordes families for sharing Roy's amazing legacy.

Chapter 2 - Ranchers & Local Folk

Roy's aviator's cap, school slate (with his handwriting still on it), and a cigar box that held marbles and other toys. His childhood stuffed animal is at top.

Krista Jenkins holding Roy's school slate, and the precious box of Roy's possessions that's been cherished by the family for three-quarters of a century.

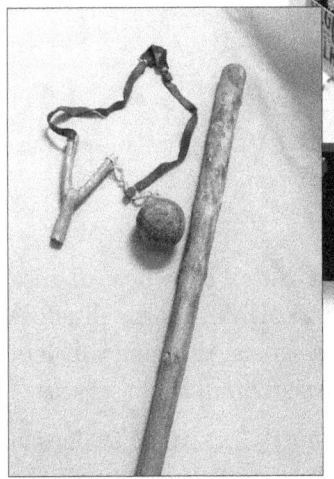

Roy's hand-carved baseball bat and well-used ball, and his homemade slingshot.

Forgotten Tales:

Earl Jepsen, in his World War I uniform (Courtesy of Douglas County Historical Society & Museum).

THE JEPSEN LEGACY

It was going to be the "War to End All Wars." But when America entered the dreaded conflict in 1917, local draft boards all across the nation were forced to make awful decisions: choosing which of their community's young men should be sent off to fight overseas.

Here in Douglas County, Nevada, County Clerk Hans C. Jepsen became one of the men tasked with serving on the Draft Board. The Board did its job in the fairest way possible: a lottery was organized, so men would be chosen at random to be drafted.

Imagine Jepsen's horror when the name that he picked was that of his own son, Earl.

Chapter 2 - Ranchers & Local Folk

According to family lore, two other men were in the room when Earl's name was drawn, and both urged Hans to simply put his son's name back and choose a different name. Perhaps they knew that Earl wasn't a likely candidate anyway, because his eyesight wasn't good. Or perhaps they sympathized with a father's guilt at sending his own son off to war.

Whatever their reasoning, Hans C. Jepsen refused. Earl's name had been chosen, and that was that.

The Army, however, wasn't quite so sure. Earl's poor eyesight was indeed a stumbling block, and they repeatedly refused to induct him. But Earl kept presenting himself for service. He wanted to help his country, he said. And eventually, the Army relented.

Hans C. Jepsen (Courtesy of Douglas County Historical Society & Museum).

Earl enlisted on June 26, 1918 and was assigned to the Infantry. By August he was overseas in the war zone in France. In late September, he was assigned to Company B of the 308th Infantry (part of the 77th Division), just in time to join them in marching into the Battle of the Argonne Forest. During this lengthy battle, Earl's company became separated from the rest of the Allied forces and found themselves surrounded by German forces. (The 554 men in these units would later become known as the "Lost Battalion.")

Earl was assigned as a runner to the battalion's field headquarters, a job so dangerous it was considered a virtual suicide mission. Earl was struck down by sniper fire October 5, 1918, while on patrol. Ironically, the Armistice would be signed just five weeks later, November 11, 1918, ending the war.

Earl was 26 years old when he fell on the battlefield. His body was buried initially in France, along with other American casualties. Three years later, thanks to funds raised here at home, his body was returned

home to the States. His remains now rest at the Presidio in San Francisco.

A memorial at the old Courthouse in Minden, Nevada features a brass plaque, honoring those from Douglas County who served during World War I. And as you will see if you visit, Earl isn't the only Jepsen to have served during this "War to End All Wars." Earl's brother, Hans R., and his cousin, Hans J., also are honored on the plaque. But the simple five-pointed star beside Earl's name signifies that he gave his life for duty.

Plaque at the old Douglas Co. Courthouse displaying the "killed in action" star beside Earl Jepsen's name. (Judy Wickwire photo).

As for Earl's father, Hans C. Jepsen, he passed away in January, 1923 in San Francisco, following an operation for stomach cancer. His funeral in Genoa was conducted by the Gardnerville Odd Fellows Lodge, of which he'd been a charter member, and was said to be the "largest assemblage that ever gathered in Douglas County to pay the last tribute that can be rendered to the dead."

By 2018, the headstone that had been erected for Hans nearly a century early had become so etched by the elements that it was virtually unreadable. The Jepsen family pulled together to set the matter right.

Grandson Tom Jepsen and his son, Harold, arranged for a new faceplate to be installed on Hans' headstone. A small rededication ceremony was held on October 20, 2018.

Next Memorial Day, we hope you will remember the Jepsens — a local boy and his father who both did what they felt they must to serve their country.

Chapter 2 - Ranchers & Local Folk

The new faceplate resting against the foot of Hans C. Jepsen's headstone just before it was installed, in October, 2018. (Judy Wickwire photo).

Grandson Tom Jepsen and his son, Harold, shared photos of their family at the rededication ceremony at Genoa Cemetery, held on October 20, 2018. (Judy Wickwire photo).

Chapter 3
WILD MEN & WILD TIMES

Chapter 3 - Wild Men & Wild Times

Luther Olds.

THE NINE LIVES OF LUTE OLDS

Think you've got problems? Carson Valley pioneer Luther Olds most likely has you beat!

Born about 1828, Luther ("Lute") Olds crossed the plains from Michigan with his brother, David, about 1850. They settled initially in Sacramento, where they found work as teamsters. Then in 1853, Lute, David, and friend "Lucky Bill" Thorington moved east again to the beautiful Carson Valley. Here, Lute recorded one of the earliest land claims on September 30, 1853 for a 320-acre ranch beside the Emigrant Trail at the foot of today's Fay Canyon, eventually building a two-story hotel there to serve passing travelers.

If things had been going fairly swimmingly up to that point, Fate took a definite wrong turn thereafter. Lute found himself embroiled in at least nine separate difficulties in the coming decades, enough to have killed or crushed the spirit of any lesser man. Among the disasters in Lute's disaster-prone life:

- A "terrible row" broke out at the Olds hotel/home during a "cotillion" dance in 1858, during which several men suffered stab wounds to their arms, backs, and hands, and women were seen hanging out the windows in horror. There were challenges, it seems, in running a pioneer hotel.

- That same year, Olds was arrested on a charge of "entertaining" horse thieves, who'd been boarding at his house or hotel. Horse-stealing was a serious crime, potentially a capital offense. Some argued that Olds deserved the same hangman's noose that had dispatched his friend, the not-so-lucky Lucky Bill. Olds, however, managed to get off relatively easily with "just" a whopping $875 fine and an order banishing him from the valley "on penalty of being shot" if he returned.

- Olds didn't stay out of trouble (or away from the valley) for very long, however. In 1860 he found himself facing charges of larceny in Judge Cradlebaugh's courtroom. So much for whatever reputation Lute might have had left.

- In 1861, a disastrous fire not only burned Olds' two-story hotel to the ground but also killed his four-year-old daughter. The little girl had been playing with matches, and Lute was said to blame himself for the conflagration and the tragedy. His wife evidently did, too; she divorced him in 1862.

- In 1870, the perpetually-ill-fated Olds just happened to be a passenger aboard the steamer "Active" when it hit a rock in heavy fog off the coast of Mendocino, during a passage from San Francisco to Victoria, British Columbia. Lute Olds and his fellow passengers were shipwrecked, but somehow managed to make it safely to the beach.

- A huge windstorm in 1873 carried off Lute Olds' barn "so clean that no one would suppose he ever had a barn." (Perhaps the barn's demise was Fate's way of clearing away bad vibes; this

Chapter 3 - Wild Men & Wild Times

was apparently the same barn where, a dozen years earlier, Henry Van Sickle had shot and killed badman Sam Brown on July 6, 1861.)

- By 1870 Lute had managed to remarry, tying the knot with a much-younger woman named Rachel Harley Smith. But in 1879, Lute's oldest daughter died of diphtheria, and that same year the couple also lost another child, an infant boy who died shortly after birth. As if that weren't enough, Olds also saw his 575-acre ranch auctioned off at a Sheriff's sale in the summer of 1879 to satisfy an unpaid debt of $7,800 to his arch-enemy, Anthony McGwin.

- Enraged by McGwin not returning personal property left behind on the now-foreclosed ranch, Olds headed back to court in 1880 to try to get his property back. Lute not only lost that lawsuit but, adding insult to injury, was ordered to pay McGwin's court costs, too.

- Wouldn't *you* have resorted to drink by now? Lute evidently did. He wrecked his buggy in an alcohol-fueled smash-up in 1881. Pieces of his buggy were reportedly found strewn "from Genoa to Walley's."

- His nine lives finally exhausted, Lute ran out of luck for good in 1882. On his way home after visiting brother David in Round Valley, Lute suffered yet another drunken buggy accident, this one proving fatal. According to the *Bishop Creek Times*, Lute had been "somewhat intoxicated" when he'd left town in his two-horse buggy at 7 p.m. Just his bad luck: the buggy overturned, not somewhere in the sagebrush, but in the waters of the East Walker River. Lute got tangled up in the traces and drowned.

Were all of these episodes bad luck or simply karma at work? Contemporary Jerome Thorington described Lute's reputation as that of "not a very honest man." And although it was never proven, Lute was long suspected of being part of a "Border Ruffian" gang that stole horses from passing emigrants, spirited them over the mountain, and resold them to oncoming wagon trains.

Adding substance to the horse-rustling rumors, the *Sacramento Daily Union* reported in 1855 that ten horses stolen from a ranch on the Jackson Road had somehow turned up on Olds' ranch. Perhaps most telling of all, nearly everyone at the ranch turned out to help arrest the horse thieves except Lute himself!

These days, no one remembers Lute Olds' many trials and tribulations. But the canyon that emerges from the mountains near the original Olds Ranch? It's still known today as Horsethief Canyon.

Chapter 3 - Wild Men & Wild Times

K. Dustman illustration.

THE MURDER OF OLD HANS

Al Livington found a nasty surprise when he stopped by a saloon in Jacks Valley the morning of August 9, 1880. There was the proprietor, face down on the floor, with a gunshot wound through the chest.

Popularly known as "Old Hans," the saloon owner's *true* name was Christopher Johannes Hull. Robbery appeared to be the motive for the crime; both Hans's large silver pocket watch and roughly $100 were missing.

It was a "murder most foul," the *Genoa Weekly Courier* pronounced. Old Hans was a "pleasant, harmless old man," noted the Reno paper. About sixty years old and nearly crippled from years of hard labor, he was "inoffensive, generous, good-natured, and the friend of everyone," the *Courier* observed.

Hans had been a miner in the early 1870s and, more recently, had worked at several stables in California and Nevada. Saving his earnings, he was able to a saloon at the north end of Jacks Valley and, just three months before his death, had sold that and moved to the little house where he was killed.

This was the Pony Saloon in Jacks Valley in 1937, showing the beautiful and remote general location. (Photo courtesy of Billie Rightmire).

Powder burns on his shirt showed the bullet had been fired at close range. In addition to the gunshot wound in his chest, Old Hans had been struck at the base of his skull by a hard object. The coroner's jury ruled it a "death by gun shot and other wounds," committed by person or persons unknown.

Hans' house stood in a "lonesome part of the valley," and no one had seen anything — or *anyone* — suspicious in previous days. But the community was incensed. Ormsby County posted a $500 reward to try to flush out the murderer.

Suspicions focused first on a local miscreant with the colorful nickname of "Buckskin Bob." According to rumor, Buckskin Bob even confessed at one point to involvement in Hans's murder. Bob proved to have a solid alibi, however, and the "pal" he supposedly confessed to couldn't be found.

By mid-October, however, Sheriff Williams and his tenacious investiga-

Suspicion focused on a local miscreant named "Buckskin Bob." (K. Dustman illustration.)

tors managed to track down Old Hans's silver watch. The watch had been sold near Sacramento by another local ne'er-do-well named Harry Fowles (sometimes spelled Fowler).

Fowles, just 26 years old, had already done a two-year stint in prison at Carson for burglary. And unlike Buckskin Bob, Fowles' account of his whereabouts on August 8 did not "hang together," as the Genoa paper smugly put it. Fowles was arrested at Rocklin, east of Sacramento, and hauled back to Genoa to face the music.

After cooling his heels in the Genoa jail for several weeks awaiting trial, Fowles outsmarted his captors: on the afternoon of November 9, 1880, he escaped. The *Genoa Weekly Courier* described how Fowles managed to pull off his escape from a brick jail cell: "He made a hole in the wall between the Jailroom and a small bedroom adjoining the Sheriff's office, crawled through, and made his way out an unbarred window on the South side of the Court House."

Harry Fowles had no good explanation for his whereabouts. (Illustration by K. Dustman)

Just what the jailer was doing that same afternoon went unreported.

Curious Genoa citizens turned out in force to inspect Fowles' route of escape. "Everybody who could get away from business immediately went to the jail," the newspaper noted. "They looked in through the hole in the wall,

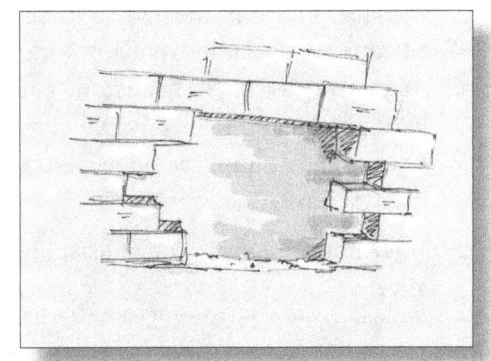

Curious Genoa citizens turned out to inspect Fowles' escape route. (Illustration by K. Dustman.)

and then they went in the jail and looked out through the hole, and went up town and knew all about it."

Sightings of the escaped prisoner soon begain trickling in from far and wide. Four days after the daring afternoon escape, the Genoa paper reported: "So far, he has been seen at Walley's Springs, Cradlebaugh's Bridge, Jacks Valley, Silver Lake, Twelve Mile House, Holbrook's, Desert Station, Woodford's, Glenbrook, Small's, Silver Mountain, Carson, Virginia, and in Roop County..."

The Genoa Courthouse from which Fowles escaped. (Courtesy of Douglas County Historical Society & Museum).

Despite all these "sightings," the paper was forced to admit that "no definite trace" of Fowles had yet been found. Nevertheless, it confidently predicted that the escapee's recapture was "only a matter of time."

Recapture, however, was not meant to be. Harry Fowles had slipped out of sight for good, and his crime (if indeed he was the one who shot Old Hans) only received proper punishment when he went to meet his Maker.

As for Old Hans, his body was "properly prepared" by kindly local citizens for burial in Genoa, where he was laid to rest on Tuesday, August 10, 1880. No headstone currently exists for this well-loved local gentleman. It's likely Old Hans was given a pauper's burial. If he ever had a simple wooden cross to mark the location of his grave, it's now long gone.

We hope this story will at least help keep the memory of Old Hans alive!

Chapter 3 - Wild Men & Wild Times

Rick Dustman photo.

A MURDERED MAN NAMED MOORE
(BUT IS HE BURIED HERE?!)

One lonely tombstone in Gardnerville's Garden Cemetery begs silently for justice. *Murdered* it proclaims in italic script, as if begging visitors to help solve the terrible mystery.

The victim, William Moore, met his awful fate sometime between the 9th and 14th of December, 1900. But the story behind Moore's demise is a tangled one indeed. Did he even really *die* that December?

Moore, 67, was evidently something of a hermit. A poor man and in poor health, he'd lived alone for twenty years in a small cabin on his ranch near the East Fork of the Carson River, above Horseshoe Bend. Here he raised horses, ran a few head of cattle, and perhaps panned for flour gold in the nearby river.

A few days before Christmas, 1900, local Indians alerted authorities that Moore's tiny cabin had burned to the ground. Sheriff Brockliss and Judge Dake promptly rode out to investigate. Not finding Moore, they searched the remnants of the charred cabin, but didn't locate any trace of a body. A day or so later, other local citizens too showed up to paw through the debris, and they, too, came up empty-handed. Possibly complicating matters was the fact that a rainstorm had gone through sometime after the fire.

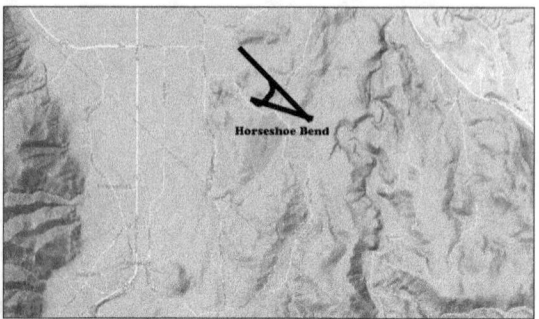

Horseshoe Bend is on the east side of Carson Valley, not far from Mud Lake.

Christmas came and went, and a few determined searchers decided to try again. On December 26 they returned, "sifted the ashes" — and came up with a few small pieces of charred *something* that might have been bone. These were carted off to Dr. Gerdes of Gardnerville, who pronounced them shards of a human skull. And when he examined one fragment more closely, "three small shot" were found to be embedded in the bone.

The local newspaper promptly dubbed this as "almost positive evidence that William Moore was murdered, and his cabin burned over his body." Dr. Gerdes opined that the bone's position could explain why the fragment was charred but the shot hadn't melted. A coroner's jury was convened, which agreeably confirmed the general belief that Moore had been murdered. Community suspicion instantly focused on "a certain Indian" named Mike Holbrook, said to have threatened Moore in the past.

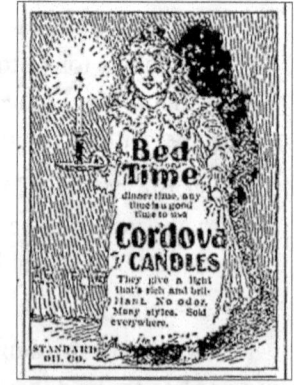

An ad for candles from the same paper that carried news of Moore's "murder." Could the fire have been accidental?

Chapter 3 - Wild Men & Wild Times

In January, the Board of Commissioners for Douglas County put out a $250 reward "for the arrest and conviction of the person or persons who murdered William Moore." That was more than enough encouragement for three enthusiastic Genoa citizens. Based on further rumors, young William Gray, accompanied by his brother-in-law Frank Walker and their friend Edgar Seamon, drove a wagon out to Mountain House in March, where they made a citizens' arrest of "Indian Mike." The local paper assured readers that this private party arrest was a "perfectly proper and legitimate proceeding," adding uncharitably that if the prisoner should later establish his innocence "he will have no one to blame but himself."

By now a new sheriff had been sworn into office and was eager to show the public his chops. The local paper expressed confidence that now-Sheriff McCormack would not only do his best to suppress crime, but "criminals have good cause to fear him." The murder case against Indian Mike became the talk of the town. The Genoa courthouse was "packed" during the two-day preliminary hearing, and "nothing was talked of on the streets but the Moore tragedy."

Several other Indians now came forward, claiming that Mike Holbrook had an alibi: he had been with them on a rabbit drive when the killing occurred. The evidence against Mike Holbrook appeared decidedly thin — except for one thing. Charlie George, also an Indian, swore he had personally witnessed Holbrook shooting Moore.

Charlie's credibility as a witness left something to be desired, however. Among other things, Charlie had been arrested the same evening as Mike on an outstanding warrant for larceny. Charlie and Mike also were said to be enemies; as the newspaper put it, "it is stated that Mike is very friendly with George's mahala."

Nevertheless, Mike was bound over for trial. The case languished for another month until April, when a new Grand Jury could be convened to issue the indictment. Friends urged Mike to take a plea bargain and admit to manslaughter in order to "save his neck." He refused.

On April 24, 1901, a jury pool of 40 local citizens was pulled, and by 3 p.m. the jury was in place. Trial began the following day, and the evidence was over by 5 p.m. Charlie George "proved a strong witness," the paper pronounced. Other "sensational" details of the case now came to light, including a "wild story" that Moore had always kept a skull in his cabin, "the victim of his rifle in former years." The newspaper hinted darkly that Brockliss, the former sheriff, had done a lousy job of investigation, sniffing that "no steps officially were taken to investigate the matter until McCormack, the present Sheriff, took office."

About dinnertime the jurors retired to deliberate, and by midnight they had their verdict: *Not guilty*. This didn't sit so well with the local paper. "And so another chapter is added to the criminal records of this county, which is not without blemish now," it chided.

As for the County Commissioners, they rescinded their earlier offer of a $250 reward for Mike's capture. Shrugged the local paper: "They have learned that a mercenary incentive for the capture of criminals does not work satisfactorily in this county."

Moore's lonely headstone in the Garden Cemetery, Gardnerville, NV. Buried here presumably are the bits of charred "bone" found at his cabin. But were they really Moore's? Or perhaps not even bone at all? (Rick Dustman photo).

Chapter 3 - Wild Men & Wild Times

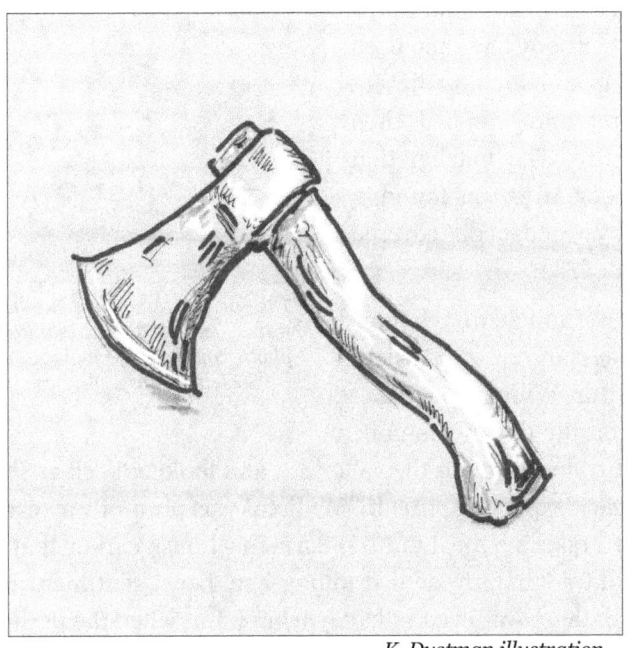

K. Dustman illustration.

THE SARMAN MURDER

The murder of 57-year-old Anna Sarman rocked Carson Valley in 1895.

Anna and her husband, Fredrick, were living on the old Ferris Ranch about four miles south of Genoa, Nevada. Like so many local ranchers, the Sarmans originally hailed from Germany; they'd arrived in the Valley in 1882, and had lived there peaceably for a dozen years before that tragic spring day. Their extended family included two married daughters and a son: Mrs. Louisa M. Heitman; Mrs. Henry Frevert; and Fred Sarman.

But May 8, 1895 would prove to be Anna's last day of life. Someone entered her home and struck Anna brutally in the head with a hatchet. Investigators reviewing the crime scene later concluded Anna had been murdered in the front room of the house; her body had then been carried to a bed in an adjacent bedroom; and the bed then set on fire. The hatchet that killed poor Anna was found in a nearby woodshed, "covered with blood."

The Sarman family lived at the old Ferris Ranch (enlarged from Juanita Schubert photo, courtesy of Douglas County Historical Society & Museum).

Nearby ranchers claimed to have spotted a transient named Jim Williams at about 3 p.m. on the day of the murder, "hurrying through the valley . . . and looking back at short intervals as if expecting pursuit." Williams was promptly arrested and admitted taking a meal at Mrs. Sarman's house earlier that morning — but adamantly denied killing her. Local sentiment initially ran high; there was even talk of lynching. But when the preliminary hearing was held, "nearly all the testimony went to show that Williams could not have committed the murder," according to the paper, and he was released.

A second transient, Joseph Richie, was arrested at Bodie about two weeks later. He, too, candidly admitted passing through Carson Valley the day before the murder. Suspiciously, he was said to wear a "narrow-toed shoe which corresponded well" to footprints found near the Sarman home after the killing. But charges against him, too, eventually were dropped.

The local rumor mill kept churning, however, and community suspicion eventually began to turn toward Anna's husband. Fritz Sarman claimed to have been out working in his fields at the time of the murder, returning home about 3 p.m. — "in the nick of time to save his property," but not to save Anna or to catch any glimpse of the murderer. Fritz claimed there were witnesses to his whereabouts during those crucial afternoon hours, but none of the witnesses he named could be found. A few townsfolk reported that Fritz had "acted strangely" after discovering Anna's body, calmly going about his usual chores and even milking his cows. Friends, however, expressed themselves "very confident" that Fritz was innocent.

When Anna was laid to rest in the Genoa Cemetery, sympathetic townsfolk turned out in huge numbers for her funeral: a reporter counted sixty wagons and buggies at the somber affair. Husband Fritz, however, did not attend; he was said to be "completely prostrated" by his wife's tragic death.

Marker for Anna Sarman at Genoa Cemetery. (Photo by Judy Wickwire.)

Husband Fredrick Sarman passed away almost exactly five years later, and is buried beside his wife. (Photo by Judy Wickwire.)

Fritz Sarman passed away on May 12, 1900, almost exactly five years to the day after Anna was killed. He, too, was buried at Genoa, right beside his wife. The mystery of Anna's murder was never officially solved.

The winds can be blustery on Genoa Lane near the Hanging Tree.

GENOA'S HANGING TREE

You may have heard the tale about Adam Uber's famous curse — uttered just before an angry Genoa mob hung him. But did you know the hanging tree itself is still there? It sits on the south side of Genoa Lane, just east of Genoa (and a conveniently short distance from the old-time jail!)

The year was 1897, and the crime began with Uber swilling Red Eye — and ended with a gunshot. Hans Anderson was dead. And Uber didn't even remember what happened when he finally sobered up in the Genoa Jail.

Anderson had been well-liked in the community; Uber was not. A group of locals decided swift justice was the finest flavor. They rushed the jail, demanded the jailer's key, and whisked Uber off for a hasty meeting with the hangman's rope.

But Uber got off a few choice last words before dropping into the Great Hereafter: he cursed those who did the foul deed "unto seven generations."

Chapter 3 - Wild Men & Wild Times

And, according to local legend, Uber's curse ultimately came true. Some of mob died sudden, violent deaths; some committed suicide; but all of them met an unhappy end. Family members, too, reportedly suffered.

They're all gone now, of course; 1897 was a long time ago. But locals say Uber's ghost can still be seen "hanging around" from time to time — either here at the tree, or at the old brick Courthouse which once held his cell.

If you decide to pay a visit to the scene of this long-ago lynching, consider making a stop at the old Genoa Cemetery as well. Uber is buried there somewhere, in an unmarked grave.

A beautiful burled tree stands silent watch nearby.

The tree where the hanging took place, with a plaque placed by local luminary Sharkey Begovich and ranch owner Arnold Trimmer. (Photos on this page courtesy of Judy Wickwire).

RIDING THE AVALANCHE.

Genoa Snowslide

Genoa, Nevada has weathered its share of disasters over the years. It's suffered through earthquakes, high winds, and of course the awful Great Fire of 1910 that nearly wiped out the town. But did you know Genoa once was struck by an *avalanche*?

The time was 5:30 a.m. on March 16, 1882. Residents who happened to be awake at that early hour heard a terrible warning rumble, akin to an oncoming freight train.

It was, indeed, a train of sorts: an avalanche of terrifying proportions came cascading down Genoa Canyon, sweeping along everything it encountered.

Main Street, Genoa, looking north. (Courtesy of Douglas Co. Historical Society & Museum).

Chapter 3 - Wild Men & Wild Times

Directly in its path was the home of Nimrod Bowers. When the snowslide finally stopped, the bodies of Bowers and his wife were found lifeless amid the snow and debris. With epic bad timing, two relatives from Germany had just arrived the previous evening for a visit. Both relatives luckily managed to escape alive, although one suffered a broken shoulder.

Bowers' barn and house were crushed, and came to rest in William Daniel Gray's kitchen at the house just below. Beams, siding, furniture and contents lay "heaped in a confusing mass," mixed liberally with hay from Gray's own mangled barn.

A native of Ohio, William Gray had been one of the earliest citizens of Genoa, arriving in 1862 and finding work initially as a blacksmith for Henry Van Sickle. Before long, Gray had opened his own blacksmith shop and was soon building buggies, spring wagons and heavy wagons across the street from the Genoa courthouse. Gray and his wife, an Irish lass named Anna, lived a house on Main Street, right next door to the lovely brick home once owned by Lucky Bill Thorington.

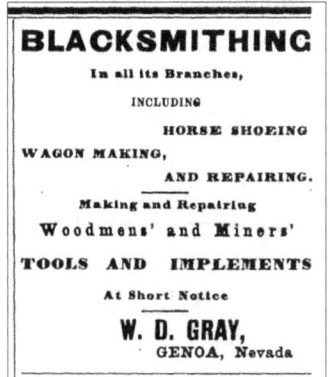

William Daniel Gray's advertisement for his blacksmith shop, in the Genoa Weekly Courier *of 1882.*

Gray was an early riser, and on that fateful March morning in 1882, he was already up and shoveling drifts away from his back door when he heard the approaching torrent. He yelled to his wife, and they managed to run toward the front of the house before the mass of snow struck, crushing the Grays' kitchen into (as the *Genoa Courier* put it) "a shapeless mass."

Miracle of miracles, not only did the Grays survive but their children, too, were spared. The kids' bedroom off the kitchen was seriously damaged, the snow coming "within a foot or two of their bed." But as old-timers today tell the tale, the children had gotten cold during the night and moved into the main portion of the house to sleep by a woodstove. Talk about lucky! Old-timers also claim at least one farm animal miraculously survived the onslaught: when the gigantic pile of snow finally ceased moving, a horse was reportedly found standing on top of the heaped-up mound!

Next door to the Grays, Judge Virgin's sturdy brick home survived the devastation largely intact, although his orchard, barn and outbuildings were flattened. But the Boerlin home on the other side of the Grays was completely demolished. Mr. Boerlin, one son, and two other occupants came through unscathed. Mrs. Boerlin was also discovered alive, still in bed, some distance away from where her house once stood, although she'd been "nearly suffocated" under broken timbers and debris. Sadly, she was clutching the lifeless body of her little daughter, Paulina, in her arms.

Behind the hedge is the Genoa home that once belonged to W.D. Gray and his wife. A corner of Judge Virgin's brick home (formerly owned by Lucky Bill) is just visible at right. (Rick Dustman photo).

Hardest hit of all was a structure farther south, occupied by several Washoe Indian families. This "long house" (as the *Courier* described it) was completely destroyed by the snow slide. At least seven Native Americans tragically lost their lives in the disaster.

Surprisingly, as workers were clearing away debris from one of the homes two weeks later, they discovered a dog beneath the broken timbers and snow. "Although it had lain cramped up for 14 days," the newspaper happily reported, "the little animal was still alive and is likely to entirely recover."

A little dog somehow managed to survive in the rubble for two weeks!

Earl Lessley (Courtesy of Marilyn Summers).

EARL LESSLEY: THE FLYING COWBOY

He died over half a century ago. But tales live on about Earl Lessley, the "flying cowboy"!

Earl Lessley was born in 1889 in Drytown, California. His parents, Mary and Samuel Lessley, had crossed the plains from Missouri by covered wagon. Even after they arrived in California, the family evidently moved around a bit; a second son, Ray, was born in 1892 in nearby Volcano.

Just how Lessley happened to mosey east to Carson Valley is unknown. But by 1918 he began working for Dangberg Land and Livestock. He would become a "veteran and respected employee" for the next 37 years. (Younger brother, Ray, may have had something to do with the move to Carson Valley; he, too, worked for Dangberg, beginning in 1919, moving on in 1937 to work for George "Bim" Koenig at the Swauger Ranch at Topaz.)

Earl's prowess as a horseman was legendary. Astride a spirited horse named "Fighting," Lessley took first prize for best rider in the finals at the American Legion rodeo in Carson Valley in June, 1928. As the years went by he would become a well-known "old vaquero" at Vaquero Cow Camp, the summer range for Dangberg cattle in Bagley Valley.

Vaquero Cow Camp in Bagley Valley, Alpine County, California. (Courtesy of Judy Wickwire).

But what Lessley was most famous for was his passion for airplanes! Given the difficulty of accessing Bagley Valley he decided to fly in with John Dangberg one winter, using a rented WW I biplane. Lessley had carefully cleared a primitive landing strip on a low ridge south of the camp. But when he attempted to maneuver in for a landing on his fresh dirt strip, the plane careened down nose-first. (Luckily, Lessley and his famous passenger both survived!)

Despite this inauspicious beginning, the landing strip at Vaquero Camp continued to be used — though not always successfully. When a second plane also crashed, the practical Lessley happily scavenged parts from the wreck to reuse on the ranch. A third pilot, too, is said to have crashed, escaping with only a broken arm. Undeterred, Earl continued to fly in, owning several airplanes of his own through-

Chapter 3 - Wild Men & Wild Times

out the years. He evidently learned from his early mistakes as a pilot; his obituary noted that Lessley "frequently had accomplished the [difficult] feat of landing and taking off from Bagley Valley."

Other near-apocryphal tales about Lessley paint a picture of a grizzled outdoorsman. Like many of his generation he disdained doctors; after developing "foot trouble" (possibly frostbite or gangrene), Lessley simply lopped off part of his own toes with an axe.

Earl Lessley's infamous biplane. (Photo courtesy of Judy Wickwire.)

Earl Lessley (left) with unknown friend in the bunkhouse at Vaquero Camp. (Photo courtesy of Judy Wickwire).

He also enjoyed a frontiersman's wicked sense of humor. Lessley once pranked local fishermen by stuffing the hind-quarters of a dead bear into a pair of old Levis, then half-buried the carcass in a river bank where he knew they would find it!

In 1952, Lessley suffered a concussion when a horse fell on him in Carson Valley. He told his coworkers to leave him there, saying he was content to die in camp. His fellow cowboys didn't listen, however, successfully carting him out on a stretcher for medical treatment.

Lessley's end came three years later — and a rather ironic end it was for an old cowboy. It was April 17, 1955, and the spring winds through Carson Valley were strong and gusty. Lessley was working on his car at the Klauber Ranch, and had jacked up the vehicle and crawled underneath. The car slipped off the jack, possibly due to the gusty wind. The rear axle landed on Lessley's chest. His body was discovered the next day by Hans Dunwebber, a fellow employee. If there was any happy news in the tragedy, it was that Lessley was thought to have died instantaneously. He was 66 years old.

The Shenandoah Valley Cemetery in Plymouth, California.

Earl Lessley was laid to rest near his parents in his family's plot at Shenandoah Valley Cemetery in Plymouth, California, in a grave he would share with his younger brother, Ray. (Ray died in 1962; it is unclear where their sister, Edith Lessley Waters, is buried.)

Earl Lessley's headstone, shared with his brother, Ray.

Prominent locals Bill Hellwinkel and Otto Heise traveled all the way from Carson Valley to Jackson to pay their respects at Earl's funeral — a touching measure of the extremely high regard in which he was held by his community.

For additional information about Earl Lessley and the vaqueros at Bagley Valley, check out Judy Wickwire's wonderful book, "Land Use Patterns in Bagley and Silver King Valleys" (Clear Water Publishing, 2017) — available at the Alpine County Museum in Markleeville, CA!

Chapter 4

BURIED TREASURE
&
A BIT OF ROMANCE

Remnants of an old fence line at what once was Double Springs.

THE STORY OF DOUBLE SPRINGS (PART 1)

There's little left today to mark the site of Double Springs, Nevada, roughly a dozen miles south of Gardnerville on Highway 395. All that's here now is a historical plaque, plus remnants of an old fence line and cattle trough. But a century-and-a-half ago, Double Springs was not only well-known — it was *notorious!*

An early hotel here beside the toll road to Aurora and Bodie offered travelers meals, beds, and pasture. A fluke of climate or simple bad luck, Double Springs became the site of several early

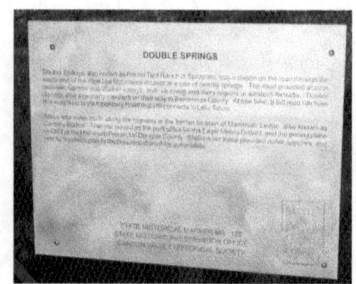
Historical marker for Double Springs.

Chapter 4 - Buried Treasure & Romance

murders. And, because all good tales include a treasure story, there's also a hidden treasure legend involving Double Springs!

The pair of springs for which Double Springs was named made this a valued spot for Native Americans back in the early-early days. Round dances were held here in both spring and fall, with prayers for the health of the pinenut trees and celebrations for abundant harvests. These huge events sometimes included as many as 500 Native Americans, and pinenut harvests could last as long as six weeks. The site's earliest recorded name, "Round Tent Ranch," may have reflected these Native American celebrations.

In 1861, rancher S.D. Fairchild claimed 320 acres here, erecting a hotel, stable, and barn. H.W. Bagley next owned the property briefly, selling it to James C. Dean about 1863. And here our tale takes a turn for the murderous!

This may be the same James C. Dean who once owned Double Springs station.

Dean was a colorful if slightly shady character who popped up in various incarnations in early Douglas County history. He and a partner bought a house and town lot in Genoa as early as August, 1860. The following year, Dean was appointed Justice of the Peace for Genoa by Governor Nye. Although ostensibly a lawyer, Dean swiftly made waves for failing to carry out the duties of his new post. Just one month after his appointment, an appeals court was forced to order Dean to do his duty; he reportedly stubbornly refused to file in papers appealing one of his decisions, and had similarly refused to send up a transcript for the higher court to consider. (The higher court was not amused.)

Despite this brouhaha, Dean's Genoa home became the site where the very first meeting of the Douglas County Commissioners was convened just after Christmas, on December 28, 1861. Dean also was honored by being elected to serve in the Nevada Territorial Legislature's House of Representatives in September, 1863, as a proud member of the Union Party.

By late 1863 Dean had moved south to Double Springs in Nevada Territory's Mammoth Precinct, a district that stretched from Teasdale Bridge on the East Carson to the southernmost edge of the county. Here he was operating his own "1st Class" Hotel and serving as a retail dealer in liquor. But Dean continued to keep an eye out for political plums. In early 1864 he penned a pleading letter to Gov. James Nye, confessing a desire to become a military man and offering to assemble a cavalry company of "burly mountain boys" if the governor would accommodate him with a commission to do so. (The governor apparently didn't take him up on this kind offer.)

Edwin Dean (possibly a cousin or younger brother of James) also briefly held elected office in early Nevada. Ed Dean served as Lyon County Treasurer in September, 1864, only to resign in disgrace a little over a year later when his books disclosed a $2,484 shortfall.

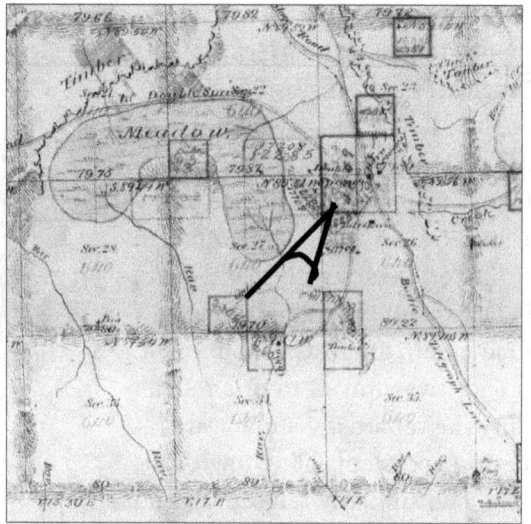

1881 map showing Double Springs at the intersection of two early roads. (Nevada Division of State Lands & UNR's DeLaMare Library).

Dean's Hotel was conveniently located at the junction of the cross-valley Olds Toll Road and the north/south Bryon's Toll Road. Travelers to Bodie or Aurora could feed their horses on hay grown at the ranch, grab a meal, or spend the night at the hotel. On December 5, 1864, Dean was also appointed to fill a vacancy for Justice of the Peace for the Mammoth Precinct. A member of the Olds family made the motion for Dean's appointment.

Chapter 4 - Buried Treasure & Romance

Sometime around 1864, however, Dean's wife, Fannie, came to a tragic end there at Double Springs station. A passing teamster found the house suspiciously quiet and, upon investigating, discovered Fannie's lifeless body. She had been severely beaten and her head was "jammed into a bucket of water." Dean was arrested by the local sheriff, but denied the murder. Dean's hotel was only about two miles from Slinkard's, and transients and travelers regularly came and went on the road by the station. As Dean pointed out, it could have been anyone who murdered Fannie Dean. Neighbors "were not satisfied with the story told," as the *Record Courier* later put it. But given the lack of evidence on which to hold him, Dean was released. Nevertheless, the story persisted for years that Dean himself had committed the murder.

By the following year, October, 1865, Dean was advertising his Double Springs property for sale. And it wasn't cheap: for the house, barn, blacksmith shop and 600 acres of land, Dean wanted $1,500, with half down and the balance in just six months. But he clearly was ready to move on; in November, 1865, he managed to get himself elected Justice of the Peace for the Walker River Precinct to the south.

Fannie's death, as it turned out, would not be the end of "notorious" murders at Double Springs. In November, 1881, another body was discovered in a small cabin about three miles south of the old station. E.A. Doud, about 65 years old, had once been an Alpine County rancher and a member of the Alpine Board of Supervisors. He'd sold his Alpine ranch about 1873, taking up residence in a 10' x 12' cabin not far from Double Springs. Roughly eight years later, his body was discovered by a Washoe Indian seeking work who had approached Doud's cabin. Looking in a window beside the door, he spied Doud's body on the floor, covered in a bloody blanket. An ax lay nearby. The Indian alerted the innkeeper at Double Springs, who in turn notified the coroner. Although a $150 reward was posted in early 1882, no suspects were ever identified.

Dean had already moved on by then. He had sold his Double Springs property to rancher P.L. Sprague about 1865 and trudged off to new adventures — and *that* quirky tale (including what happened to Dean's second wife) is our *next* story!

As for the famous Double Springs Hotel itself, the building was torn down in the fall of 1887. Its lumber was hauled off to a mining settlement overlooking Smith Valley known as South Camp, where (as the *Genoa Courier* put it), the materials were used "to cover the mill and to build a mansion for the miners."

*Continue reading for **Part 2** of this story — what became of James Dean (and his second wife)? And in **Part 3**, the tale of a hidden treasure at Double Springs!*

View from Double Springs today looking west.

Chapter 4 – Buried Treasure & Romance

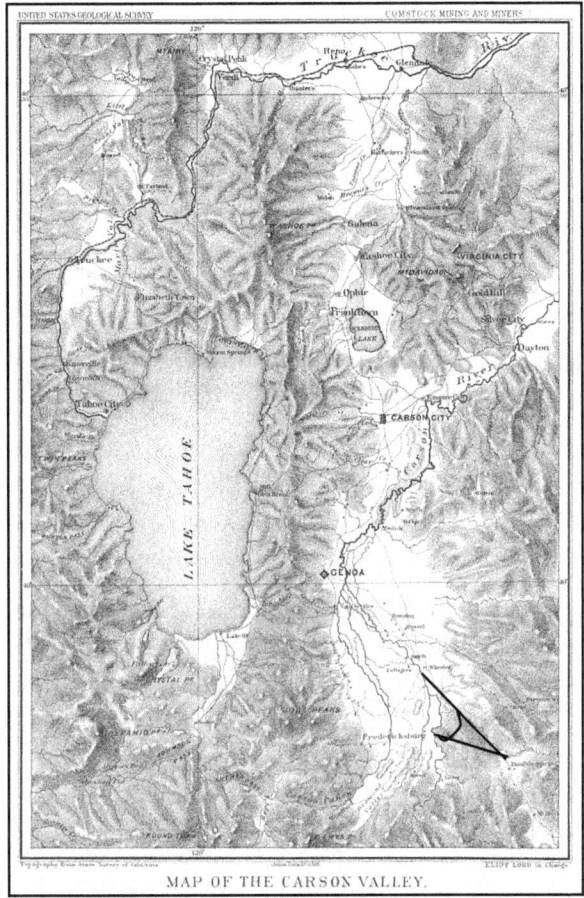

Early map, showing Double Springs at lower right.

THE STORY OF DOUBLE SPRINGS
(PART 2)

So, whatever became of James Dean?

No, not *that* James Dean. We're talking 1864. As we saw in Part 1, the person who murdered Fannie Dean at Double Springs Ranch that year wasn't much of a mystery — at least as far as the neighbors were concerned. Fannie's husband, station-keeper James C. Dean, was quickly whisked into custody by the authorities. But proof was another matter.

As the suspect pointed out, the Station was on a well-traveled road; riff-raff came and went. It could have been anyone who stuffed poor Fannie Dean's head into a bucket of water!

With no definitive evidence to tie him to the murder, Dean was eventually released. Might there have been other reasons for Dean's get-out-of-jail-free card, as well? It's hard to know, 150 years later. But our guess is that Fannie's demise occurred *after* her husband was named Mammoth District Justice of the Peace — if only because a murder suspect wouldn't normally be anyone's top pick for an open judicial post. As a local notable, was Dean perhaps able to pull a string or two?

However it happened, Dean was once again a free man. But local minds hung onto their suspicions. It was an opportune time for Dean to (as they say in the Westerns) get out of Dodge. And get out he did.

Not long after Fannie's death, Dean ran for Justice of the Peace in the nearby Walker River precinct, winning the election in November 1865. That same October and November, Dean was advertising his Double Springs Station for sale in the *Douglas Banner*, and he soon found a buyer: rancher P.L. Sprague (Sprague, in turn, would sell the Double Springs ranch to T.B. Rickey in 1883 and move on to Sheridan).

So, whatever became of James C. Dean once he left Double Springs? Traces of his trail are few and far between, but we did manage to pick up a few breadcrumbs.

Dean turns up in Hamilton, White Pine County, Nevada, in April, 1869, marrying a second wife, Theresa Dirks. Theresa was a savvy divorcee with a mind of her own — and, perhaps especially appealing for Dean, property of her own. Theresa owned real estate in both San Francisco and Hamilton City, Nevada, plus a boardinghouse and home in Virginia City (located at 90 South D Street and 91 South C Street respectively).

Theresa may have had her doubts about Dean from the get-go: she took the precaution of recording a formal marriage contract. That document confirmed that Dean consented to Theresa maintaining

Chapter 4 - Buried Treasure & Romance

control of her property, acknowledging it had been "acquired by her own unaided industry." (In case you're wondering about Theresa's earlier history, she had been married initially to Leonard Dirks in San Francisco. She became an early inhabitant of Virginia City, showing up in 1860 among the throngs at the first Christmas Ball in Storey County with her daughter, Leonora.)

But Theresa's second husband, Dean, wasn't cut out for marriage, it seems. He and Theresa were divorced in February, 1872, just three quick years after their wedding. Theresa may not have been the steadiest of marriage partners either; she remarried yet again on June 3, 1872, only a few months after divorcing Dean — making it her third marriage.

Was Dean something of a smooth-talker, blessed with the gift of gab? We may never know for sure. But in his early life, he was a lawyer, if that tells you anything. Yet another suggestion that his tongue may have been well-oiled comes from Dean's later profession: by 1873, he was operating an auction business in Pioche.

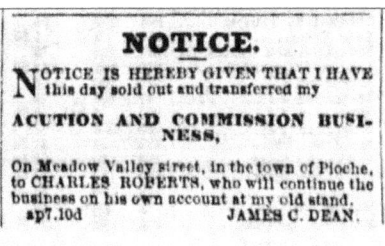

Dean ran an "Auction and Commission" business in Pioche, which he sold in 1874.

In 1880, Dean shows up in Eureka, Nevada, again working as an auctioneer. He's listed as single, and is sharing a house with E.H. Dean, the same ne'er-do-well relative whose accountings were found somewhat less than satisfactory when he served as Lyon County's treasurer.

Dean's ex-wife, Theresa, and her third husband, Robert Charles (a banker), were back in Virginia City by this time, residing in her house at 91 South C Street. Theresa died that

Theresa Dirks and her daughter, Leonora, are buried at Virginia City.

same year (1880), and is buried using her first husband's name (Dirks) at the Silver Terrace Cemetery, along with her daughter, Leonora.

As for Dean — unfortunately, it's a common enough last name that it hasn't been easy to track his remaining years. Nevertheless we did turn up a "James Calhoun Dean" who moved from the west coast back to Michigan about 1908. This James C. Dean died March 10, 1910 in Plymouth, Michigan from cancer of the head and "general senility."

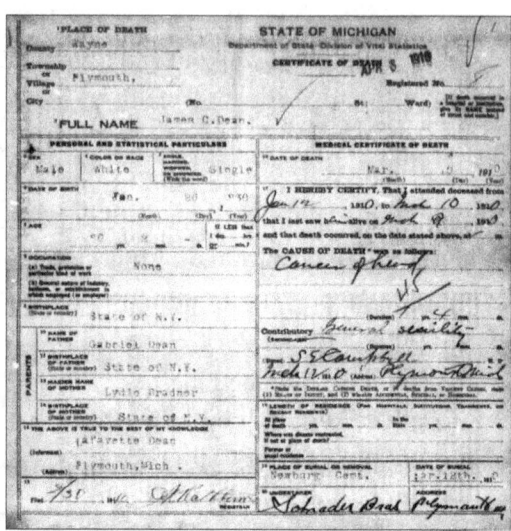

Death certificate for a James Calhoun Dean who died in 1910.

If "our" J.C. Dean is the same man, this would be a picture of the infamous Double Springs proprietor himself! There are definite similarities besides the common middle initial: both men were born in New York; their birth years roughly match; and James Calhoun Dean had been out west before returning to Michigan.

For now, at least, we'll leave the possibility that this is our Double Springs Dean in the "good guess" category.

Just possibly "our" James C. Dean of Double Springs.

But the best part of the Double Springs story is yet to come in **Part 3** — a stagecoach robbery . . . and a buried treasure!

Chapter 4 - Buried Treasure & Romance

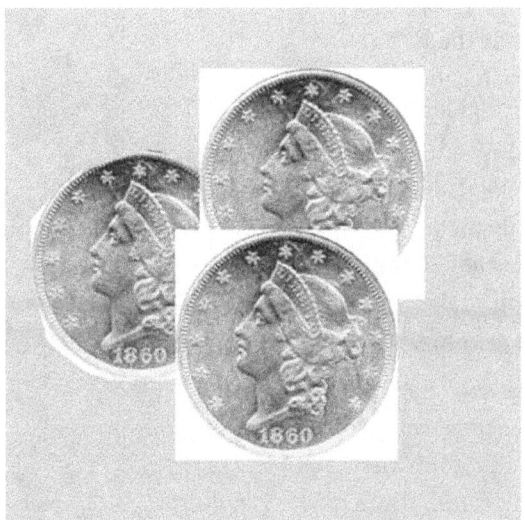

Is there hidden treasure near Double Springs?

THE STORY OF DOUBLE SPRINGS (PART 3)

It was 1863 when a lone highwayman stepped out to stop the stage near Double Springs, Nevada. Whether it was sheer luck or courtesy of an inside scoop, the robber hit payday: the heavily-laden coach was carrying some $17,000 in gold coin on its route between Aurora and Carson City.

Naturally, the robber couldn't get far hauling all that heavy gold. But like all good criminals, he'd thought ahead: he brought along a shovel. And *somewhere* in the flats not far from Double Springs, the robber dug a hole and buried his loot.

The authorities, of course, were soon hard on the robber's heels. Before long, the bandit found himself cooling those heels in Nevada's state prison. There he finally died. And according to legend, although the robber kept his secret almost to the end, on his death-bed he finally described the spot where he'd buried all that loot he couldn't take with him into the next life.

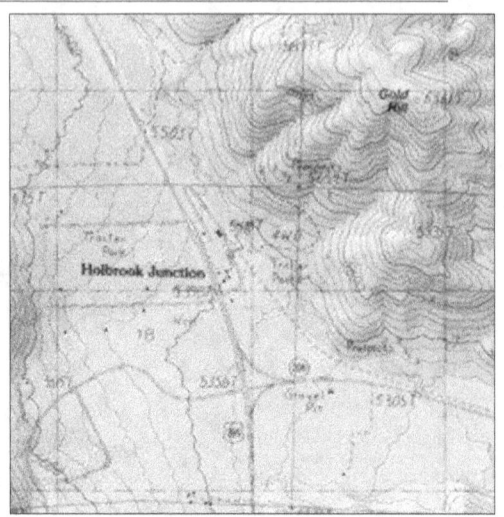

The robber told listeners that the spot where he'd buried the gold was near a small cabin south of Double Springs, roughly a mile and a half north of another old way station known as Mountain House.

Mountain House was a way station just north of today's Holbrook Junction. Today, a rest stop on the west side of Highway 395 occupies the spot where this way station once stood.

Many looked for the robber's treasure over the years, but none have yet found it — and not for lack of trying! "The ground in the vicinity looks like an artichoke patch deserted by a drove of swine," remarked the *Genoa Weekly Courier* in 1891.

In 1891, Genoa resident Henry Rice "saw" the spot where the treasure was hiding in a dream. Dragging along friend William Parsons and several young ladies for company, he eagerly rushed out to find the spot. The prospectors' hopes were soon dashed when they discovered that there were, sadly, "a hundred places that looked just like the one revealed in his dream." By way of consolation they continued on south to Walker River, where they settled for the 'treasure' of a grand picnic lunch.

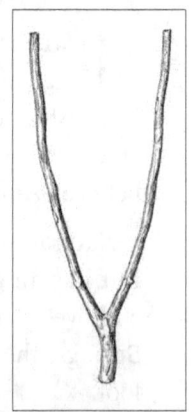

Others, too, would try their hand at finding the robber's loot through the years. One local named George Dale was said to have "dug up a good-sized

Charley Holbrook used a divining rod to try to locate the treasure.

Chapter 4 - Buried Treasure & Romance

ranch in the vain effort." Charley Holbrook was so convinced his divining rod had pinpointed the loot that he dug a 28-foot deep shaft before concluding at last that he must be in the wrong spot.

All of which is, presumably, *good* news for modern-day treasure-seekers. If you believe the old legend, the lost stagecoach gold must still be out there, somewhere not far from Double Springs!

(Gentle reminder: It's not 1891 anymore! Please don't trespass or go digging unless you get permission from the property owner first!)

Forgotten Tales:

STAGE ROBBERIES & WELLS FARGO'S FINEST - PART 1

Did stage robberies still occur as late as 1893? Just ask poor Mike Tovey; he died in one.

Okay, this technically isn't a Carson Valley tale. But it does involve the Bodie & Carson Stage – and another buried treasure that just might be somewhere in Northern Nevada!

The headstone of Mike Tovey stands its silent vigil in the Jackson City Cemetery. It was erected by his employer, Wells Fargo & Co., which evidently felt a bit guilty about Tovey's death.

Our story begins back in 1880, when Tovey was hired to guard the Bodie and Carson Stage. That stage, it seems, was in dire need of guarding, having risen high on the "frequent flyer" list for stage robbers. The coach was first robbed on June 4, 1880. Three months later, it was robbed again. Eventually the line accrued what may be a world's record: six separate stages robbed in under four months,

Chapter 4 - Buried Treasure & Romance

with as many as 20 robberies occurring elsewhere throughout the region! The whole robbery thing became, as one news article put it, "monotonous."

Victims reported that two robbers worked the hold-ups in tandem. One robber was said to be a true gentleman: well-dressed and unfailingly polite to unfortunate passengers riding the stage. The other robber — well, *not so much*. Victims described *his* voice as gruff and his manner as frightening.

Wells Fargo assigned one of its best guards to the job: Mike Tovey. Tovey came well-equipped for stage protection. A giant of a man, he stood over six feet tall, was described as 'big,' and had a reputation for being utterly fearless.

Handsome Wells Fargo guard "Mike" Tovey had wavy hair and a full beard. Born in Canada on Feb. 4, 1842, his real first name was Martin.

Sure enough, on September 5, 1880 while Tovey was on stage-protection duty, two men stepped out to hold up the Bodie and Carson Stage yet again, this time about seven miles from Aurora. Tovey managed to shoot one of the would-be robbers, taking a return bullet in the arm himself.

As Tovey was being whisked off to a nearby farmhouse to have his bullet wound attended to, a second Wells Fargo guard scoured the nearby sage for traces of the remaining bandit. But while pursuers were out beating the bushes looking for him, "the robber doubled on his tracks, returned to the stage, and carried off the treasure box" — with $700 inside. Talk about a cool customer!

Wells Fargo, of course, was now more eager than ever to track down the villain — not to mention recover its money. Trained investigators were assigned to the task. These helpfully observed that the dead robber (the one Tovey had shot) had been wearing a peculiar "mask made of red morocco leather." A clue worthy of a Sherlock Holmes himself!

Unfortunately, the dead robber's body got buried before investigators ever thought to check the man's pockets . . . but when they *did* think of it, they belatedly had the body exhumed again. Sure enough, there in the dead robber's pockets was important evidence: a bank passbook showing the man's name, a recent deposit of $1,000, and the address of a rooming house on Minna Street in San Francisco.

The dead robber could now be officially identified as W.C. "Bill" Jones, *aka* Frank Dow. A felon who'd already served time at San Quentin, Jones (Dow) had been known for his heavy drinking, large beard, and scary-sounding voice.

Armed with the helpful address, Wells Fargo's investigator now had no difficulty tracking the dead man to his former haunt in San Francisco. Detectives descended on the boarding house and searched his room (apparently not bothering with a search warrant). Lo and behold, a gold watch, ring, and other jewelry taken during the June stage robbery were found. Adding to the mounting evidence: swatches of morocco leather were also turned up, similar to the leather of the dead robber's mask.

Jones' fellow robber — the one who'd coolly made off with the cash box — was arrested at the same boarding house when he showed up a few hours later to "recover his valise." Or at least, the authorities *assumed* it was the second robber. As soon as the suspect entered he was taken to the floor, a pair of pistols oleveled at his head, and his belongings examined.

His name, the man told deputies, was Milton Anthony Sharp. Newspaper accounts make Sharp sound as if he had just stepped out of the pages of a novel: he was "remarkably fine-looking," with "jet-black hair, swarthy complexion," a goatee and black mustache, not to mention "eyes that shine so brightly that it is impossible to distinguish their color." A few lady readers may have swooned.

Milton A. Sharp.

The man suspected of being the gentleman bandit who robbed the stage — and wounded Tovey — was a debonnaire character named Milton A. Sharp.

Sharp had the bad luck when arrested to be carrying an astronomical $2,400 in cash, plus other valuables. Naturally he claimed he had come by it all honestly while working as a

Chapter 4 - Buried Treasure & Romance

miner. But like his roommate, the dead robber, Sharp had also made a bank deposit on the very same day in the very same bank, similarly listing Minna Street as his address.

Sharp was hauled off for trial at Aurora, where he was convicted of five counts of robbery and sent to cool his heels in State Prison for twenty years. There, the gentleman bandit was described by fellow prisoners as the "chief aristocrat in their midst." Or so the *Pioche Record* proclaimed in December, 1880.

But Sharp had a few tricks up his sleeve: he managed to escape incarceration not just once, but twice! While awaiting trial he tunneled his way out of the Aurora jail, taking off with a 15-pound ball-and-chain still attached (later found smashed against a rock). Sharp was quickly recaptured and quickly sent off to prison, but nine years later, he managed to escape his prison cell, too.

Four years after this second escape, Sharp was still on the run when *someone* shot Wells Fargo guard Mike Tovey for the second time, as he guarded a stage headed for Jackson. And this time, the wound to Tovey proved instantly fatal.

Was the murderer Sharp? Tune in for the rest of the story in Part 2 of this tale!

MICHAEL TOVEY.

STAGE ROBBERIES & WELLS FARGO'S FINEST - PART 2

It was June 15, 1893 on a remote stretch of road outside Jackson, California. Mike Tovey was again riding shotgun as a security guard for Wells Fargo, this time aboard the stage heading from Ione into Jackson. Mike had been shot once before in his dangerous career; no doubt his eyes were scanning the countryside for possible trouble.

As the stage crested Morrow Grade that fateful day, the vista was open — hardly the sort of territory where a highwayman would be expected. And that's exactly when a man clad in blue coveralls stepped out from behind a small clump of buckeye bushes — and, without warning, fired directly at the stage.

Tovey toppled forward. A bullet had ripped its way through his heart. Fearless Mike Tovey, "one of the strongest, biggest and most cheerful shotgun messengers in the employ of the Wells Fargo Ex-

Chapter 4 - Buried Treasure & Romance

press company that ever rode through the lonely mountain passes of the Sierras," was dead.

Suspicion promptly centered on Milton Sharp, of course — Tovey had been instrumental in sending Sharp to Nevada State Prison for a series of stage robberies in 1880. After several failed attempts to escape, Sharp had finally successfully broken out of prison in 1889, and had been on the run for four years before Tovey was shot. Rumor was that Sharp had recently sent threatening letters to Tovey — or at least *someone* had, using Sharp's name.

The hunt for Milton Sharp was on. He was soon captured in Red Bluff, California by a sharp-eyed police officer who recognized his "wanted" picture.

But somehow the sweet-talking bandit managed to convince authorities he wasn't the one responsible for Tovey's killing. And although he still had a sentence to serve for his original stage robberies, Sharp had already finished nearly half his twenty-year sentence. He managed to talk Wells Fargo into recommending a pardon for his earlier crimes, claiming he'd been "rehabilitated" during his years on the run. Sharp won a formal pardon in 1894 and was released from custody. For the rest of his life he remained on the right side of the law — or so they say, anyway.

So ... Sharp was never convicted of Tovey's murder. Instead, a petty crimi-

The dead messenger.

"Fearless" Mike Tovey was dead.

Milton A. Sharp.

The hunt for Milton A. Sharp was on.

nal named Bill Evans confessed to the crime. Well, he offered up a confession to it, anyway. Today's lawyers would cringe to hear that he did so without benefit of a lawyer being present. Evans would later say he'd been drugged and set up by an over-eager sheriff and a cooperating stool pigeon. Even the press anticipated a "not guilty" verdict at Evans' trial due to the large volume of what one newspapermen carefully termed "conflicting evidence." None other than Wells Fargo's own detective was convinced Evans wasn't guilty.

It actually took *two* criminal trials. But three hours into deliberations after the second trial, a jury finally voted to convict. Evans was sentenced to spend the rest of his life in prison — for a murder he may or may not have committed.

So did Evans really shoot Tovey? Or did Sharp, Tovey's long-time enemy, not only exact revenge for being sent to prison but also get away with murder?

And one other mystery: whatever happened to Milton Sharp's robbery loot? Treasure-hunters are convinced that Sharp and his partner must have buried a good bit of their treasure. Estimates vary about how much was taken during the pair's estimated 20 stage robberies. Some say it came to $6,000 (in 1880 dollars); others claim it could have been even more.

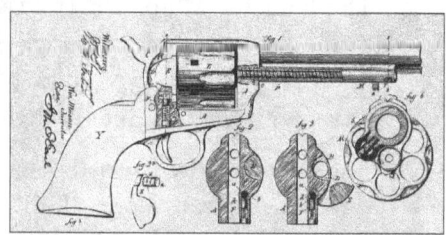

So who actually shot Wells Fargo guard Mike Tovey?

Small portions of the loot were reportedly found in 1910 by a pair of treasure-hunting brothers named Hess. Wouldn't we all love to know where the rest might still be hiding.

P.S. If you're ever at the Jackson City Cemetery, we hope you'll pay a visit to Mike Tovey's grave. It's not far from the tall monument of Zacharius Kirkwood, which is easy to spot with its large round ball.

Chapter 4 - Buried Treasure & Romance

The forgotten grave of Wells Fargo's "shotgun messenger" Mike Tovey at Jackson City Cemetery.

Headstone of Zacharius Kirkwood with its large ball on top (worth visiting in itself!) makes a great landmark. Tovey's grave is not far away.

Frances Williams and her husband, D.R. Jones (courtesy of Douglas County Historical Soc. & Museum).

THE FIRST SETTLER WEDDING IN CARSON VALLEY

The year was 1854 when two young riders pulled up outside Henry Van Sickle's blacksmith shop astride a single horse.

Their arrival at Van Sickle's station wasn't all that unusual — "Van" (as locals knew him) was an in-demand blacksmith and wheelwright, and his trading station had become a popular stopping place for emigrants.

Henry Van Sickle's Station.

What was unusual, however, was the mission of the two riders. Young David R. Jones and his even younger companion, Frances

Chapter 4 - Buried Treasure & Romance

Angeline Williams, weren't interested in Van's assistance as a blacksmith, but rather his help as a Justice of the Peace. They'd just eloped together on horseback, and wanted Van to marry them.

Frances was a native of Pennsylvania who'd come west with her family by wagon train, arriving in Carson Valley during the fall of 1853. David had been born in Wales in 1830, emigrating as a child with his family to Wisconsin. David, too, had followed his dreams west to Carson Valley in 1853 as a member of the same wagon train as the Williams family, and was living and working on the ranch owned by Frances' father*, William T. "Billy" Williams.

Still clad in his leather blacksmith's apron and rolled-up shirtsleeves, Van Sickle performed the briefest of ceremonies.

David was 25 years old when he rode up to Van Sickle's blacksmith shop that fateful day. Frances, on the other hand, was just 15. And they hadn't asked her parents' permission to get married.

As later writers recounted the tale, "Van" was hard at work at his forge when the eager young couple rushed in. Still clad in his leather blacksmith's apron and rolled-up shirtsleeves, Van Sickle obliged with the briefest of ceremonies. Clapping one meaty hand on David's shoulder and the other on Frances', he solemnly proclaimed: "As Justice of the Peace of this township, I pronounce you man and wife under the law of the Territory of Utah." That was it. They were married.

It was the first settler marriage ever performed in Carson Valley, at least according to local legend. (Small pause for a word of caution: when it comes to "firsts" like marriages and babies, there can often be room for dispute! But that's how local legend tells it.) And the Jones' wedding wouldn't be Van Sickle's last. In August, 1857,

Van Sickle also "stopped branding cattle long enough to perform the marriage" for Elzy Knott and Mary Harris.

There's just one small factual hiccup giving later historians pause about the long-ago Jones wedding story: Henry Van Sickle probably wasn't actually a J.P. yet in 1854. It wasn't until Carson County, Utah Territory was formed in September, 1855 by Orson Hyde that Henry officially became a judge, as nearly as we can tell. Prior to that, although J.P.'s did exist, their authority was limited to handling court cases. With no authority vested in anyone at the time to perform weddings, emigrant marriages were sometimes accomplished by written "contract" or by stretching the fictitious jurisdiction of an eastern J.P.

Still, the story of the Jones' wedding is so detailed there's likely some truth to the tale. Perhaps the young couple believed Van Sickle had the power to marry them, and Van simply tried to oblige. Maybe later tellings got the year wrong and the marriage took place in 1855, after Henry really was a Justice of the Peace. Or maybe the well-respected Van Sickle was simply the closest thing anyone had to a J.P. in those early days, and local folk never questioned the well-intentioned marriage attempt.

However it happened, if the oft-repeated story about the early wedding is true, newlyweds David and Frances must have had quite an interesting conversation with her family when they finally returned home to the Williams ranch! But any hard feelings were apparently soon forgiven. David would later purchase the Williams ranch in 1857.

The couple's first son, John R. Jones, born in 1855, was reportedly the first white male child born in Carson Valley. All told, David and Frances would go on to have a total of eleven children. One of those children, daughter Sarah, grew up to marry Lorenzo Smith of Washoe City. (Daughter Sarah was laid to rest at the Washoe City Cemetery in early 1894.)

David was (or at least, later claimed to be) the first to plow the ground with an ox team near Genoa, and soon began hauling hay and grain to Virginia City. But the early years of their marriage were filled with the dangers and difficulties of early pioneers. He would

Chapter 4 - Buried Treasure & Romance

later recall: "We hid in the willows at night, [my] wife and I, because the Indians were hostile in those days and we feared for our lives."

Over the years the Jones ranch grew, and by 1882 was valued for tax purposes at $3,500. David evidently developed a passion for fine horses. In 1878, the newspaper reported a price of $10 for breeding services by his "noble-looking" stallion, Westfork.

David Jones was an active member of the local community, officiating as a judge of elections at the Mottsville Precinct in 1880, and serving as a Douglas County commissioner in the

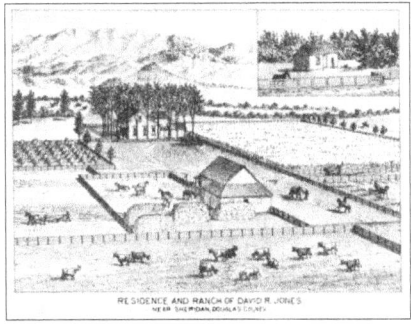

The prosperous Jones Ranch as it appeared about 1881.

D.R. Jones' "noble" stallion, Westfork, was described in the Carson Valley News *of April 12, 1878.*

1890s. According to some accounts, Jones also became a prominent and well-respected member of the Mormon Church — although in actuality, he'd broken ties with the LDS church. Instead, Jones may have been affiliated with the Reorganized Church of Jesus Christ of Latter-day Saints when that movement emerged in the 1870s, although the nature of his association with the group remains unclear. In any event, Jones was listed as a "minister" at the marriage of John Boston and Nettie Jones in March, 1872, and was kindly referred to as "Rev. Jones" in February, 1898 when he officiated at the funeral of Mrs. Mary Gilman.

Frances passed away in 1909, with seven of her 11 children still surviving her. Five years later, in 1914, David was applauded as the oldest still-living Nevada pioneer at the state's 50th anniversary celebration. He died that same year, at the age of 85.

David and Frances Jones are both buried in the historic Genoa Cemetery.

* Note: *William T. Williams was identified as Frances' father in Sam P. Davis's later* History of Nevada *(Vol. II), but according to letters in the possession of descendants, her real father was actually David Williams. It's possible that William T. Williams was an uncle.*

Special thanks to the Douglas County Historical Society for the account of David and Frances' elopement, in a typescript of the reminiscences of Robert A. Trimmer in the Van Sickle Library collection. A similar story about the Jones wedding was recounted by Owen E. Jones in the Record-Courier of September 4, 1925. David Jones' account of hiding in the willows was reported in the Record-Courier of February 5, 1909, and his land purchase from "Bully [probably Billy] Williams" was in the Genoa Courier, December 19, 1902. The account of "Rev." Jones conducting the funeral of Mrs. Gilman is from Genoa Weekly Courier, February 11, 1898.

And just a quick acknowledgment: I am so thankful for the help of local historians who know so much more and so freely share! Many thanks to one local historian in particular (who prefers to remain nameless) for the great information about the date of Van Sickle's election as Justice of the Peace, various early marriage hurdles and work-arounds, and David Jones' still-not-quite-clear connection with the Reorganized Church of Jesus Christ of Latter-Day Saints.

Chapter 4 - Buried Treasure & Romance

Unidentified 1955 press photo of Kay Williams and Clark Gable. (from DearMrGable.com).

CLARK GABLE & MINDEN'S OLD-TIME JUDGE

Clark Gable was a true gentleman. And we have that on the very best authority: straight from Minden's own early Justice of the Peace, Walt Fisher. One of Fisher's very first acts as JP was to perform the 1955 marriage of the much-married Gable to actress Kay Williams.

The Douglas County Clerk pulled a bit of a fast one when Gable and Williams showed up to apply for a marriage license. It was after hours, so she dialed up Judge Fisher and asked if a couple could come to his home to be married. "Fine," he said. "Send them over." The clerk didn't bother to mention who she was sending. So imagine Fisher's surprise when he opened his door!

The couple had brought their own witnesses with them, so there was no need to call Fisher's wife from the other room. Gable was quiet — a true gentleman, Judge Fisher later recalled. The service was quickly over, and Gable tucked $500 in the judge's hand as the newlyweds departed. The judge's wife didn't learn who had been in her house until several minutes after they'd left (an omission for which the judge, it was said, later paid dearly!)

It was Gable's fifth marriage, and Kay's third. Perhaps it was Judge Fisher's special touch; this marriage stuck, lasting until Gable died in 1960. And as for Judge Fisher's own story, that's a fun tale in itself!

Walt Fisher was born in 1885, on a Colorado ranch adjoining the famous Calgary Ranch. Walt's father was killed in a tragic ranching accident when Walt was just a boy, leaving his mother a widow — and a pregnant one at that. Next-door rancher Calgary had recently lost his own wife in childbirth, so the solution was obvious: Calgary and Mrs. Fisher were soon married, combining households, ranches and children.

G.W. "Walt" Fisher, East Fork Justice of the Peace. (Photo courtesy of granddaughter Teri Balfour).

This new arrangement was tough on Walt, however; his step-father, he felt, was "too much of a disciplinarian." So at 16 Walt struck out on his own, working his way west as a hired hand on cattle and sheep drives. Walt and a brother eventually arrived in Virginia City about 1906. There they opened a bakery together — an occupation that Walt continued to love all his life. His grandchildren still remember his homemade sourdough bread, biscuits and pancakes.

Mining in Virginia City hit a downturn, and Walt moved to Carson City. There he found employment as a freight engineer for the V&T Railroad at the

An early view of the V&T Station in Carson City, where Walt Fisher began his career with the railroad.

Chapter 4 - Buried Treasure & Romance

Carson Station, beginning in 1910. And there he also found — love.

In Carson City, Walt met pretty Alice Taylor, a young seamstress. Alice had come west by wagon from Illinois as a teenager with her widowed mother and three sisters, and together they had opened a tailoring shop in Carson City about 1910. Alice and Walt met when he came into her shop — and were married in 1913.

Walt continued to work for the V&T and in 1924, secured a position as the new Minden stationmaster. The small wooden terminal at Minden included a branch post office, a pot-bellied stove, and a large pickle jar. Local ranchers would come in to get their mail, hang around the woodstove, and (of course) talk. Walt soon knew everyone in town.

But around 1950, word came that the Minden station was going to be shut down. Walt had worked for the V&T for a total of over 40 years, and was ready for something new.

Alice and Walt Fisher with their two children, Lois and Franklin. (Photo courtesy of Teri Balfour).

The early depot at Minden. To the right is the stationmaster's home. (Courtesy of Teri Balfour).

Walt had once rescued a young Basque from being beaten by local thugs, earning him the respect of the local Basque community. Hearing that Walt was about to retire from his position with V&T, local Basques approached Walt to offer support if he would run for

Justice of the Peace. And the rest, as they say, is history. Walt ran successfully for the office in 1954, eventually serving four consecutive terms in office as East Fork Justice of the Peace.

Walt and Alice lived on Mono Avenue, across from the old brick Elementary School in Minden. It's the same modest home where Gable and Williams arrived in 1955 to be married. And it's *also* where one very drunk female driver was hauled by officers at 4:30 in the morning, after she'd backed her vehicle from a bar right into a parked car.

Given the wee hour, Judge Fisher answered his door clad in a black bathrobe. There stood the arresting officers with the inebriated woman — so inebriated she mistook Fisher in his black bathrobe for a Catholic priest. Once assured that the judge was not a priest, she berated him for *impersonating* a priest.

Walt and Alice's home on Mono Avenue. (Photo courtesy of Teri Balfour).

The woman proved too tipsy to face the legal music even hours later, when the court's regular session began. As the *Record-Courier* reported, the ever-patient Judge Fisher ordered "another 24 hours free lodging in the calaboose."

And with that plus a $100 fine, justice was served.

Walt's wife, Alice, passed away in December, 1960, after a lengthy illness. Walt continued to serve on the bench until poor health finally forced his retirement in 1961. He passed away in 1963. Walt and Alice are buried at Lone Mountain Cemetery in Carson City, their joint headstone a sweet reminder of their fascinating lives together.

A Word To Our Readers:

Well, this is not *really* the end. New bits and pieces of history keep turning up, and we hope to eventually add a "Volume 2" to this series! If you have additions or corrections for this book, or better yet, *new* stories to tell us about the fun history of Carson Valley and its surrounding communities, please reach out! We'd love to hear.

Here's where you can get in touch:

Clairitage Press

www.Clairitage.com

Kdustman@Clairitage.com

And if you loved this book, we hope you will tell your friends!

Here's to History!

Index

A

Accidents 24
Adams brothers 65
Adams, Ellen 64, 66
Adams, Elsie 68
Adams family 58, 68
Adams, John Elias 66
Adams, John Q. 64, 66
Adams, Katie 68
Adams, Mary Lydia 66, 67, 68
Adams Ranch 64, 65
Adams, Rufus 64, 65, 66
Adams, Rufus W. 68
Adams, William Rufus 66, 68
Ahern Ranch 55
Airplanes 118, 119
Aja family 40
Allen & Dake 55
Allen, Richard 20, 22
Allerman children 48
Alpine County, CA 11, 48, 61, 62, 71, 125
Alpine County Supervisors 125
Al Tahoe Pioneer Cemetery 30
Andersen's Hay Yard 10
Andersen, Zirn 10
Anderson, Hans 112
Arbor Day 54, 56
Armstrong, W.J. 70
Arnot, Eugenia 48
Arnot, N.D. 48
Auction business 129
Aurora, NV 124, 135, 137
Avalanche 114, 115, 116

B

Bacon, Ted 72
Bagley, H.W. 123
Bagley Valley 118, 119, 120
Bakery 148
Baldwin, Elias Jackson 6
Baldwin Hotel & Theatre 6
Baldwin, Lucky 6
Banishment 98
Bar 23
Barley 65

Barns 70, 71, 85, 98
Bartels children 48
Basques 149
Battle of the Argonne Forest 93
Beef 24
Begovich, Sharkey 113
Behrman, Tante 89
Bently Ranch 78
Berning children 48
Berning, Henry 76
Berning, Ina 77
Berning, Mina 77
Berning, Nina 77
Berning triplets 77
Berning, Viola 76, 77
Beste, Henry 37, 47
Biplane 118, 119
Blackburn, Abner 18
Blacksmiths & blacksmith shops 23, 37, 38, 70, 115, 142, 143
Bodie and Carson Stage 134, 135
Bodie, CA 124
Boerlin family 116
Boerlin, Paulina 116
Bohlman, Albert 25
Bohlman boys 55
Bohlman, Dale 25
Border Ruffian gang 99
Boston, John 145
Bowers, Nimrod 115
Boyd Toll Road 73
Brick 58, 64, 65, 66
Brockliss, Sheriff 106, 108
Brown, Sam 99
Bryon's Toll Road 124
Buckskin Bob 102
Buggy 85, 99
Buggy accidents 99
Buried treasure 121, 123, 126, 131, 132, 140
Butter 7, 9, 10, 32, 33, 80

C

Cabins 18, 81, 106, 125
Calaveras Big Trees 30
Cancer 94, 130

Index

Cardinal, Bertha Dangberg 49
Carson Canyon route 18
Carson City, NV 7, 10, 22, 23, 75, 76
Carson County 19
Carson Valley 20, 24
Carson Valley Creamery 6, 8, 9, 32
Carson Valley Inn 9
Carson Valley Museum 90
Cary, John 69
Cattle 81
Cavanaugh, Nellie M. 55
Cemeteries 57, 58, 105, 129, 134, 144
Chalmers, Lewis 12, 61, 71
Charles, Robert 129
Cheese 7, 9, 10
Childs, J.S. 66
Chinese 28
Christmas Ball 129
Christmas celebration 47
Church 52, 70
Citizenship 84
Civil War 74
Clift, F.D. 81
Close, Perry (Dr.) 31
Cohn, E. 6
Comstock Lode 20
Cordes, Chris 85
Cordes, Marieken (Thran) 85
Courthouse 44, 65, 94, 103, 104
Cowboys 117
Cradlebaugh, Judge 98
Cradlebaugh Road 73
Creameries 6, 7, 8, 9, 32, 33
Creamery process 9, 10
Cress, John 53
Crosby Ranch 55
Cushing, Hattie (Harriet) 48, 49

D

Daggett, Dr. Charles 19
Daggett Pass 17, 19, 20, 22, 23
Daggett Trail 19, 20
Dairy ranches 7, 8, 22, 70, 86, 89
Dake, Bert 15
Dake, Charles (son) 12
Dake, Charles W. 11, 12, 13, 15, 16
Dake, Harriet 15
Dake House 11, 12, 13

Dale, George 132
Dam 89
Dances 65, 98
Dangberg, Bertha 49
Dangberg children 48, 75
Dangberg, Fritz (*nephew*) 10
Dangberg, Grace 75, 76
Dangberg, H.F. "Fred" (Sr.) 75, 76, 79, 80, 81, 82, 83
Dangberg, H.F. (Jr.) 32, 34, 43
Dangberg Home Ranch 75, 79, 82
Dangberg, John 118
Dangberg Land and Livestock Co. 117
Dangberg, Margaret Gale (Ferris) 75, 76, 77
Dangberg, William 7
Daudel, Albert 44
Dean, Edwin 124, 129
Dean, Fannie 125, 127, 128
Dean, James C. 123, 124, 125, 126, 127, 128, 129, 130
Dean, Theresa (Dirks) 129
Decoration Day 60
Depression 58
Diamond Valley, CA 59, 62
Dieckhoff, Marie 85, 87
Diphtheria 99
Dirks, Leonard 129
Dirks, Leonora 129, 130
Dirks, Theresa 128, 130
Divining rod 132, 133
Dixon, Henry 38
Doctor 13, 19, 39
Dog 116
Dolan, Ellen 66
Double Springs, NV 122-127, 130-131, 132, 133
Double Springs Station 128
Doud, E.A. 125
Douglas Banner 128
Douglas County Clerk 92, 147
Douglas County Commissioners 107, 108, 123, 145
Douglas County "D" 74
Douglas County, NV 24, 42, 43, 44, 94
Dow, Frank 136

153

Draft board 92
Dressler boys 55
Dressler Lane 85, 86, 89
Dressler, William 32, 43
Drowning 90
Dunwebber, Hans 120
Dutch Creek, NV 67

E

Eagle Valley 82
East Fork Justice Court 43
East Fork of the Carson River 80, 82, 105, 124
East Fork School 46, 47, 48, 49
East Fork School District 46
Edwards, William 83
Electrification 39
Elges, Henry 49
Ellis, John and Norma 49
Emigrants 23, 99, 142, 144
Emigrant Trail 18, 65, 97
Empire, NV 55
Enlow, Elizabeth (Peters) 28
Evans, Bill 140
Ezell, L.S. 43

F

Fairchild, S.D. 123
Fairview Rd. 53
Fairview School 51, 52, 53, 55, 56
Fairview School District 55
Falcke, Carl (Sr.) 60
Farmers' Mill 25
Fay, George (Mrs.) 49
Fay-Luther Canyon 51, 53, 97
Felch, Leroy 35
Ferris family 74, 76
Ferris, Fred 74
Ferris, George W.G., Sr. 74, 75, 76, 77
Ferris, G.W.G., Jr. 75, 77
Ferris, Harriet 74
Ferris house 75, 76, 77, 78
Ferris, Margaret Gale (Dangberg) 75
Ferris, Martha 74
Ferris, Mary 76
Ferris Ranch 73, 75, 76, 109, 110
Ferris Wheel 75
Field, Mary 55

Fire 40, 44, 52, 98, 106, 110
First Records 19
Fischer, Michael 35
Fisher, Alice 149, 150
Fisher, Franklin 149
Fisher, Lois 149
Fisher, Walt 147, 148, 150
Flume 21, 23, 24
Folsom's logging camp 24
Foothill Road 17, 69
Fowler, Harry – *see* "Fowles"
Fowles, Harry 103, 104
Franklin, L.T. 13
Frantzen children 48
Frantzen, John 7
Fredericksburg, CA 9, 82
Fredericksburg Road 54
Frevert, Mrs. Henry 109
Frey family 13
Fricke, Fred 37
Fricke, Richard 33
Friday's Station 23, 27
Frostbite 19
Fulstone, Bob 22

G

Gable, Clark 147, 148, 150
Garden Cemetery 105, 108
Gardnerville Branch Jail 42, 44, 45
Gardnerville Hotel 36
Gardnerville Laundry 49
Gardnerville, NV 36, 37, 38, 42, 43, 49, 105
Gardnerville Odd Fellows Lodge 94
Gardnerville School 48
Gates, Bill 7
Genoa Brewery 22
Genoa Canyon 114
Genoa Cemetery 16, 57, 58, 59, 67, 68, 77, 95, 104, 111, 113, 145
Genoa Courthouse 44, 65, 103, 104, 107, 113, 115
Genoa Jail 103, 104, 112
Genoa Lane 112
Genoa, NV 11, 12, 19, 20, 21, 43, 44, 70, 82, 103, 112, 114, 123
Genoa School 66
Genoa Weekly Courier 9, 14, 36, 38,

Index

54, 66, 101, 103, 115, 126, 132, 146
George, Charlie 107
Georgetown, CA 18
Georgetown Cutoff 18
Gerdes, Dr. 106
Ghosts 11, 12, 14, 15, 113
Gilman, Mary 145, 146
Globe Mine 12
Goddard, George 19
Gold Canyon, NV 80
Gold Country (Calif.) 17
Gold mining 80
Gold Rush 18, 28, 33, 74, 80
Gossi, Joe 60
Granary 43
Gray, Anna 115
Gray, William D. 107, 115, 116
Greenbacks 74
Green, Mr. 24
Grog shop 28, 29

H

Haddock, Jack 35
Haines, J.W. (Sen.) 24, 69
Haines Ranch 69
Halloween 53
Hand-sleds 24
Hanging 83, 112
Hanging Tree 112, 113
Hanke, Henry 85, 86
Harris, Mary 144
Hawkins, E.H. (Dr.) 39
Hawkins, George 7
Hawkins, Harry 12, 83
Hawkins, Leander 71
Hawkins, Theodore and Clara 13
Hay 65, 70
Headstones & wooden markers 58, 59, 61, 68, 94, 95, 120, 141
Heath, Fred 81
Heise, Fritz 7
Heise, Otto 120
Heitman, Louisa M. 109
Hellwinkel, Bill 120
Henke 85
Henke – see Hanke
Henningsen, C.C. 7

Henningsen, C.M. 7
Hess brothers 140
Hinde, Edmund 18
History of Nevada (Sam P. Davis) 146
Hobart 25, 31
Holbrook, C.E. 82
Holbrook, Charley 132, 133
Holbrook Junction 132
Holbrook, Mike (Indian Mike) 106, 107, 108
Hope Valley 22
Horses 145
Horseshoe Bend 105, 106
Horsethief Canyon 100
Horse thieves 98, 99, 100
Hotels 23, 27, 30, 31, 36, 37, 38, 39, 40, 70, 97, 98, 122, 124, 125, 126
Hull, Christopher Johannes 101, 102, 103, 104
Humboldt & Salt Lake Telegraph Co. 21
Humboldt-Toiyabe National Forest 31
Hussman children 48
Hussman, Emma 49
Hyde, Orson 19, 144

I

Ice house 39
Imperial Silver Quarries 61
Indian Mike (Holbrook) 107, 108
Ives Survey Map 28, 29, 31

J

Jackson, CA 138
Jackson City Cemetery 134, 140, 141
Jacks Valley, NV 52, 53, 101, 102
Jacobsen children 48
Jacobsen, Jennie 49
Jacobsen, Minnie 49
Jailbreaks 103, 104, 137
Jails 42, 43, 44, 45, 103, 104, 112, 137
Jenkins, Krista 90, 91
Jennison, Emma 47, 48
Jepsen, Earl 92, 93, 94
Jepsen, Hans C. 36, 92, 93, 94, 95
Jepsen, Hans R. 94
Jepsen, Harold 94, 95

Jepsen, Tom 94, 95
Jimmy Allen Flying Club 89
Johns, Abednego 52, 53
Jones, David R. 142, 143, 144, 145, 146
Jones, Frances (Williams) 142, 143, 144, 145, 146
Jones, John R. 144
Jones, Nettie 145
Jones, Owen E. 52, 146
Jones Ranch 144, 145
Jones, Sarah (Smith) 144
Jones, W.C. "Bill" 136
Jubilee Ranch 69, 70, 72
Juchtzer, Arnold 60
Judges 43, 48, 55, 123, 124, 125, 128, 143, 144, 146, 147, 150

K

Katie's Restaurant 9
Kaupisch brothers 7, 8
Kaupisch, Julius 7
Kiln 58, 65
Kingsbury Canyon 24
Kingsbury, D.D. 20, 22
Kingsbury Grade 17, 18, 21, 22, 24, 25, 26, 27, 28
Kingsbury & McDonald Toll Road 20, 21, 22, 23, 24, 28, 29, 31
Kingsbury Road 17, 23, 24, 29
Kings Canyon 23, 24
Kirkwood, Zacharius 140, 141
Kiwanis Club 26
Klauber Ranch 81, 83, 120
Knott, Elzy 144
Knott, Thomas 83
Koenig, George (Bim) 118

L

Lake Bigler Road 23
Lake Tahoe 24, 29
Lamb, Miss 55
Land claims 81, 82
Lapham, Frances Marion 29, 30
Lapham, William W. (Capt.) 30
Larceny 98
Latter-Day Saints 52
Laundry 49, 50

Layne, Ella S. 51, 55
LDS Church - *see also* "Mormons" 145
Lenwick, Louis 25
Leslie, Belle 55
Lessley, Earl 117, 118, 119, 120
Lessley, Edith 120
Lessley, Mary and Samuel 117
Lessley, Ray 117, 120
Lindbergh, Charles 89
Livery stable 37, 38, 39, 40
Livington, Al 101
Lloyd, Miss 54, 55, 56
Lone Mountain Cemetery 40, 77, 150
Lookout point 26
Lost Battalion 93
Lucky Bill - *see* Thorington
Lutheran Church 88, 89
Luther Pass 22
Lyon County Treasurer 124

M

Mammoth Precinct 124, 128
Mapes, Charles 55
Marotz, Dr. 39
Marriages 143, 144, 145, 146, 147
Marsh Ranch 85
Martin, Jack and Maria 86, 87
Mast, Benjamin 80, 82
Mathews, Henry 37
McCord, Julia 48
McCormack, Sheriff 107, 108
McDonald, John M. 20
McGwin, Anthony 99
Meat wagons 71
Medical doctors 39
Memorial Day 60
Merrick, C.E. 7
Meyers 25
Middle Fork of the Carson River 82
Minden Butter Manufacturing Company 32, 33
Minden Co-Op Creamery 33
Minden Creamery 32
Minden depot 39, 149
Minden Elementary School 150
Minden, NV 32, 43, 44, 147, 149
Minden Park 34

Index

Minden School 88
Minden School District 55
Mindens - other states 33, 34, 35
Mining 61, 67, 102
Monitor, CA 12
Mono Avenue 150
Moore, William 105, 106, 107, 108
Mormons 19, 52, 53, 145
Mormon Station 18, 19, 20
Morrow Grade 138
Mottsville Cemetery 72
Mottsville Lane 17
Mottsville Precinct 145
Mountain House 107, 132
Muller Lane 17, 74
Murders 76, 101, 102, 105, 106, 107, 109, 110, 111, 123, 125, 127, 128, 137, 140

N

National Register of Historic Places 11, 42, 44, 45
Native Americans 145
Nelson, Chris 37
Nelson, Hans 36
Nelson, William 49
Nevada Secretary of State 74
Nevada State Capitol building 76
Nevada Territory 123, 124
Nevin, Kate 48
Nishikida family 50
Nishikida laundry 49, 50
Nixon Street 70
Nixon, William 19, 20
Noteware, Chauncey 74
Novacovich, J. 55
Nye, Governor James 123, 124

O

Odd Fellows 94
Oka, George 49
Old Hans 101, 102, 103, 104
Olds, David 97, 99
Olds family 124
Olds hotel 98
Olds, Lute (Luther) 97, 98, 99, 100
Olds, Rachel Harley (Smith) 99
Olds Ranch 100

Olds Toll Road 124
Opium 13
Organ 47, 51
Outhouses 55

P

Pack trains 22
Park, H. 43
Parsons, William 132
Peters, Clara 30
Peters, Elizabeth 23, 28, 30
Peters' Flat 28, 30, 31
Peters, Frances (Lapham) 30
Peters, Richard 23, 28, 29, 30
Peters, Richard M. (son) 29, 30, 31
Peters' Station 23, 27, 28, 29, 30, 31
Pettegrew, Ida 48
Pioche, NV 129
Pioche Record 137
Placerville 18, 21, 23
Plymouth, CA 120
Pony Express 21, 28
Pony Saloon 102
Post office 149
Premonition 89
Prisoners 43, 44, 103
Prussia 79

R

Rabbit drive 107
Ranching 24, 149
Record-Courier newspaper 34, 38, 47, 49, 125, 146, 150
Reorganized Church of Jesus Christ of Latter-Day Saints 145, 146
Reward 107, 108, 125
Rice, Henry 132
Richie, Joseph 110
Rickey, T.B. 128
Ritchford, Anna 38, 40, 41
Ritchford family 37
Ritchford Hotel 36, 37, 38, 39, 40, 41
Ritchford, William 36, 37, 38, 39, 41
Ritchford, William (Jr.) 40
Robb, Alex 28
Robbery 131, 134, 135, 137, 138
Robishaw children 48
Rodenbah children 48

Rodenbah, Sue 49
Rodeo 118
Roosevelt, President 67
Round dances 123
Round Tent Ranch 123
Round Valley 99
Rowland's Station 30
Ruhenstroth boys 55

S

Sacramento, CA 23, 24
Saloon 28, 29, 36, 101, 102, 124
Salt Lake City 20
Sanborn Fire Insurance map 38-40
San Francisco 10, 14, 15
Sarman, Anna 76, 109, 110, 111
Sarman family 110
Sarman, Fred 109
Sarman, Fredrick (Fritz) 76, 77, 109, 110, 111
Sattler, John 33
Sauquet, John 61, 62
Sawmill 30
Schacht, Fritz 33
Scheele, Herman 9
School bell 47
Schools 46, 47, 51, 52, 54, 55, 66
Schrantz, Scott 39
Schubert, Juanita 73, 77, 110
Schwake Ranch 89
Schwarz, A. 22
Scossa, Agnes (Thompson) 59, 62
Scossa, John 62
Scott, J.H. 18, 19
Seamon, Edgar 107
Seamstress 149
Sears-Ferris House 75, 76
Sears, Gregory A. 75
Selkirk, Bert (Mrs.) 49
Settelmeyer children 48
Sharp, Milton Anthony 136, 137, 139, 140
Sheep camp 78
Shenandoah Valley Cemetery 120
Sheriff's sale 99
Shingles 25
Shingle Springs 22
Shipwreck 98

Shooting 99, 101, 137
Sierra Nevada 23
Silver Creek 62
Silver Mountain City, CA 11, 12, 61
Silver, Sue 31
Simonis, John 16
Simpson, Capt. J.H. 20
Skunks 55
Slaves 19
Slinkard's 125
Small & Burke's Station 23
Smith, Lorenzo 144
Smith, Minnie Jacobsen 49
Smith, Rachel Harley 99
Smith, Sarah (Jones) 144
Smith Valley, NV 126
Smoke Shop 47
Snowslide - *see* "Avalanche" 114
Snowstorm 25
South Camp, NV 126
Spencer, Mr. 52, 55
Spirit painting 14
Spooner's Station 23
Sprague, P.L. 125, 128
Springmeyer children 48
Springmeyer, H. 7
Springmeyer, Louis 42
Stage 134, 135, 138
Stage robbers 131, 134, 135, 138, 139
Stage stops/Stations 70, 127, 128
Stockyard Road 73, 78
Store 49
Stores 23
Summers Ranch 72
Summers, Thomas 72
Surveys 19, 28, 29, 81, 83
Swauger Ranch 118
Syll children 48

T

Taft, President 67
Taylor, Alice (Fisher) 149
Taylor, Carl ("Fiddler") 58
Taylor, Katie 55
Teachers 47, 48, 51, 55, 66
Teamsters 23, 27, 31
Teasdale Bridge 124
Telegraph 21

Index

Thompson, Agnes 59, 60
Thompson, John A. ("Snowshoe") 57, 59, 60, 61, 62
Thorington, Jerome 99
Thorington, William (Lucky Bill) 79, 81, 82, 83, 97, 98, 115, 116
Thran, Carl 85, 86
Thran, Dietrich (Dick) 84, 85, 86, 88
Thran, Emma 85
Thran family 86
Thran, Herman 85
Thran House 84, 86, 89
Thran, Marie (Dieckhoff) 85, 86, 87, 88, 89, 90
Thran, Mariechen (Cordes) 85, 89
Thran, Richard 85
Thran, Roy 88, 89, 90
Tierney, May 48
Timber 30
Token 33
Tolls 22, 23, 24
Topaz, CA 118
Tovey, Mike 134, 135, 137, 138, 139, 140, 141
Traders 80
Tramps 76, 110
Trees 54, 56
Trimmer, Arnold 113
Trimmer, Robert A. 146
Triplets 77
Trunk 84, 87
Tucke Ranch 85
Twelve Mile House 47

U

Uber, Adam 112, 113
Undertaker 12, 13, 15
U.S. Mint 65
Utah Territory 143, 144

V

Valhalla Hall 7, 38
Van Sickle, Henry 23, 24, 69, 70, 71, 75, 99, 115, 142, 143, 144, 146
Van Sickle, Lillies 70, 71, 72
Van Sickle, Oscar 72
Van Sickle, Peter 31, 69, 70, 71, 72

Van Sickle Station 22, 70
Van Sickle Toll Road 24
Vaquero Cow Camp 118, 119
Virgin, Ellen 55
Virginia City, NV 10, 20, 22, 23, 65, 128, 129, 145, 148
Virgin, Judge 55, 116
V&T Railroad 39, 148, 149

W

Wagon train 143, 149
Walker, Frank 107
Walker Lake Indian Reservation 67
Walker River 99
Walker River Precinct 125, 128
Walley, David 58
Walley's Hot Springs 58
Washoe City Cemetery 144
Washoe City, NV 144
Washoe Tribe 18, 76, 106, 116, 123, 125, 145
Waterloo Lane 6
Waters, Edith Lessley 120
Water tower 37, 41
Water well 55
Way station 23
Weddings 142, 143, 144, 146
Weingardt, Richard G. 76
Wells Fargo 134, 135, 137, 138, 139, 140, 141
West Fork of the Carson River 89
Wheeler, Thomas 47
Wickwire, Judy 120
Wilder, Pete 37
William Moore 105
Williams, David 146
Williams, Delbert E. 66, 67
Williams family 67, 143
Williams, Frances (Jones) 142, 143, 146
Williams, Jim 110
Williams, Kay (Gable) 147, 148, 150
Williams Ranch 144
Williams, Sheriff 102
Williams, William T. (Billy) 143, 146
Wilslef family 47
Wilslef, Peter 47
Winkelman, Metta 10

Woodstove 51, 52
World War I 60, 92, 93, 94

Symbols

20-30 Club 26

www.ingramcontent.com/pod-product-compliance
Lightning Source LLC
Chambersburg PA
CBHW050553300426
44112CB00013B/1896